HOW TO MARKET DESIGN CONSULTANCY SERVICES:
Finding, winning and keeping clients

The Design Council is the UK's national authority on design. Its main activities are:

- commissioning research on design-related topics, particularly stressing design effectiveness to improve competitiveness;
- communicating key design effectiveness messages to industry and government; and
- working to improve both design education and the role of design in education generally.

The Design Council is working with Gower to support the publication of work in design management and product development. For more information about the Design Council please phone 0171-208 2121. A complete list of book titles is available from Gower Publishing on 01252 331551.

HOW TO MARKET DESIGN CONSULTANCY SERVICES:

Finding, winning and keeping clients

Shan Preddy

Gower

Published by
Gower Publishing Limited
Gower House
Croft Road
Aldershot
Hampshire GU11 3HR
England

Gower
Old Post Road
Brookfield
Vermont 05036
USA

Shan Preddy has asserted her right under the Copyright, Designs and Patents Act 1988 to be identified as the author of this work.

British Library Cataloguing in Publication Data
Preddy, Shan
How to market design consultancy services : finding,
winning and keeping clients
1. Design services – Marketing
I. Title
729'.0688

ISBN 0 566 07727 2

Library of Congress Cataloging-in-Publication Data
Preddy, Shan.
How to market design consultancy services : finding, winning and
keeping clients / Shan Preddy.
p. cm.
Includes index.

ISBN 0-566-07727-2 (cloth)

1. Design services—Europe—Marketing. 2. Design services—
Europe—Management. I. Title.
NK1173.P74 1997
745.4'068'8—dc21   96–46415
                                    CIP

Typeset in Garamond by Bournemouth Colour Press, Parkstone and printed in Great Britain at the University Press, Cambridge.

My grateful thanks go to the many advisers and practitioners who have generously contributed to this book; to all of my clients who either buy or sell design services and who have told me in no uncertain terms over the years which aspects of marketing work, and which do not; to Andrew Birch and to *Design Week* for their kind permission to reprint some of the cartoon strips 'The Designers' about the exploits of an imaginary design consultancy; to my assistant Sandra Beaumont-Pike and to the editors at Gower, whose eagle eyes have prevented many an interesting and inventive grammatical and typographical error; to Suzie Duke, the commissioning editor, without whose ideas this book would never have been started; and to Don Preddy, my husband, without whose continual support and encouragement it would never have been finished.

CONTENTS

PART II THE PRACTICE: HOW IT IS DONE **125**

Leading European practitioners share the secrets of their success

FOREWORD

In an increasingly competitive world, design companies face continuous pressure to invent new ways to win. They need to position themselves appropriately so that clients know of their special skills, creativity and effectiveness – not simply of their existence. They need to differentiate themselves. They need to develop short- and long-term marketing strategies. And they need to do all this ethically and responsibly.

But the very nature of design companies is to spend most of their time, energy and resources worrying about their clients' needs – not their own. It is hardly surprising that many of them find it difficult to market their own services successfully. Smaller companies can rarely afford to employ marketing specialists and the bigger ones have to carefully weigh the need to invest in marketing against a variety of other pressing demands.

Knowledge is the key. New knowledge is needed to help design companies find their own individual approach to marketing – designed to suit their particular situation, size and strengths. This book is a rare contribution to this need as it brings together a collection of ideas, insights, anecdotes and practical information, providing a wealth of material to stimulate thinking, planning and action.

John Sorrell

INTRODUCTION: WHY YOU NEED THIS BOOK

'It isn't that they can't see the solution. It is that they can't see the problem.'
G K Chesterton, *The Scandal of Father Brown*

The task of marketing your own services is no longer an optional activity. In the current competitive economy, no design company will survive for long, let alone grow and develop, without an effective marketing programme.

Fifteen or 20 years ago, it was quite possible to launch a successful design company by following a very simple three-point strategy:

1 Obtain a client from existing personal or business contacts, by convincing them that your design services will bring them commercial results
2 Do excellent work for them
3 As a result:
   i Enjoy further commissions from that first client
   ii Be approached by additional clients acting on the first client's recommendation

As long as you consistently repeated from step 2, you could watch your business grow organically, and fairly rapidly.

This is exactly how many of our longest-established design companies started, and it remains the case that the consistent provision of excellent work, excellent value for money and, increasingly, excellent service will build your business more securely than any amount of publicity or promotional activity.

Easy? Can you stop reading now? Well, not quite. Nowadays, we are faced with a completely different market situation, full of the hurdles of credentials presentations, competitive tenders and creative pitches, both paid and unpaid. We work in an increasingly overcrowded marketplace: the supply of design services worldwide far outstrips the demand. Instead of clients struggling with the problem of sourcing a consultancy, as they did in the past, the consultancies struggle with the problem of sourcing clients. In common with all oversupplied markets, this increases the need for design companies to have powerful marketing campaigns. You need to convince potential clients that you are the very best consultancy for the job.

This book has been written to help you to develop the best possible marketing strategies and plans. It is divided into two parts.

● Part I is 'The Principles: How to do it'. This consists of 12 chapters containing practical information and advice on the different stages of marketing design consultancy services. The names of the people and companies used in the illustrative examples throughout the book are, of course, purely fictional and bear no relation to any actual people or companies. At the end of each chapter, you will find a series of cumulative activity exercises which you can complete either on your own or with a group of colleagues. The activities have been developed so that you can apply the thinking outlined in the book to your own company and situation. As with so many aspects of business, the theory is actually very simple. It's putting it into practice that can prove to be troublesome. Between the chapters, you will find contributions from several experienced advisers to the design community – the consultants to the consultants.

- Part II is 'The Practice: How it is done'. This contains the edited transcripts of interviews with some of Europe's leading design practitioners. One of the most interesting discoveries is the variation in approach taken by each company: a successful method for one consultancy is often dismissed as a waste of time and effort by another. They have all striven to find a way which works for their own situation, and they have all succeeded. However, it is clear that none of these companies stands still as far as its marketing activities are concerned: in 12 months' time, each might tell a different story.

If you are just launching a new design consultancy, this book contains all you need to know about the marketing of your services. If you are responsible for marketing a much more established company, it will encourage you to take a critical look at your current methods and to learn some new ones. No matter how large or small your company, nor which design discipline you specialize in, this book can help you to improve your marketing skills.

PART I

The Principles: How to do it

1 GETTING STARTED

'All things are difficult before they are easy.'
Ancient Persian proverb

- The basic requirements of a marketing programme
- What is marketing?
- Product-focused or market-focused?
- Where has your business come from?

The basic requirements of a marketing programme

How do you put together a workable marketing programme for your company? Regardless of your budget or the scale of your programme, you will need to:

1   Know where your current business has come from, and understand which aspects of marketing have worked for you in the past.

2   Know what your overall company objectives are. Where do you want to be in one, five and ten years' time? Have clear objectives for your marketing programme, based on your overall company objectives. What exactly are you trying to achieve?

3   Understand the general purchasing criteria for design, and what clients look for when thinking about buying design consultancy services. What is your marketplace like?

4   Know what you can offer. What do you do? The word 'design' is no longer sufficient on its own: we work in far too diverse an industry. As well as identifying your core activity, you will need to establish a strong and defendable positioning for yourself, by working out where you stand in relation to your closest competitors.

5   Identify a precise target market or markets for your own services. Who wants you?

6   Develop competitive propositions or sales benefits which will help to persuade a potential client to appoint you rather than another company, and which will encourage existing clients to stay with you. Why should they bother?

7   Consider the different approach methods you might use to reach these potential clients. How will they find out about you?

8   Put together an implementation plan with timings and budget and resource allocations.

9   Make sure that you are completely consistent in your communications, visually as well as verbally, and that you use a tone of voice which is appropriate

both to you and to potential clients. Buyers listen best to voices speaking their language, but it is also important that all of your promotional activities reflect your own company's personality.

10 Identify the resources you have available. Be flexible. The mainstay of your activities should be based on strategic marketing, with a sustainable programme aimed at developing long-term fee income from new and existing clients. However, tactical opportunities will often occur, where you will want to respond quickly to an immediate opportunity, and it is important to allow yourself the option of tactical actions where appropriate or necessary.

11 Work on your credentials presentations, written tenders and competitive pitches so that your success rate improves. The writer Flaubert once said that prose should be combed and combed until it shines. Comb your presentations carefully.

12 Finally, make sure that once you have gained a client, you do not let them go. The book deals with each of these subjects in turn, starting with a look at your current business profile. First, though, let's take a quick look at marketing in general.

What is marketing?

Marketing is not simply another word for selling. As a skill, selling forms a part of the marketing process – and a very important part – but it is not the process itself.

In his book *Management*, Peter Drucker gives this as a definition: 'The aim of marketing is to make selling superfluous.' By this, he means that if you have done your marketing well, clients will come to seek you out. This is true. If you read the interviews with leading design practitioners in Part II of this book, you will hear several of them say that they are in the enviable position of receiving unsolicited briefs from both existing and new clients. Their main problem seems to lie in deciding whether or not those briefs fit the long-term strategic direction of their companies. How did they achieve this utopia? Through careful marketing. How do they maintain it? The same answer.

Drucker's definition builds on economic views held since the last century, when it was believed that all you had to do was to develop the best possible product and sales would automatically follow. This is perhaps best exemplified in the words of the 19th-century American, Ralph Waldo Emerson, in his often-quoted statement: 'If a man write a better book, preach a better sermon, or make a better mousetrap, though he build his house in the woods, the world will beat a path to his door.' To an extent, this is still true; an inferior product will not sell. Not twice, anyway.

However, the competitive nature of business-to-business communications at the end of the 20th century is such that it is no longer enough to have talent as your sole asset, however good your end-product might be. The quality of your work will always determine your future success but, however established you are, you still need to do more than sit back and wait for the commissions to come in. You need to let prospective clients know (a) that you exist, (b) what you are offering to do for them, (c) who else you have done it for, and (d) what makes you different from – or better than – other design consultancies, so that they appoint you and not the others. Then you have to keep reminding them. Today, I suspect that Emerson's mousetrap maker would simply starve to death in his little arboreal cottage.

Product-focused or market-focused?

In traditional marketing circles, a great deal has been written about the need for companies and organizations to be market-focused, and not product-focused. The essential difference is that a product-focused company would say: 'We provide this item or service, so we need to work out a way to sell it to someone.' A market-focused attitude would be: 'Let's find out exactly what people want, so that we can offer them something that they will want to buy from us.'

Most design companies believe that they are market-focused but, in practice, many are product-focused. They tend to try to sell their existing services to potential clients, rather than think about developing those services to meet clients' continually changing needs. It has frequently been said that the only thing you can rely on in business to be constant is change itself.

This product-focused attitude results in significant problems for the design companies concerned. They can become inward-looking and their communications, both spoken and written, with potential clients deal with themselves and their own interests instead of actively demonstrating that they are listening to the potential client's concerns.

Product-focused companies carry on trying to sell the same old service to both existing and potential clients, often for years. They fail to look for ways to improve their offer. It is only when commissions start to dry up or they see that their clients are taking work to competing design consultancies that they lift their heads over the parapet, scan the horizon and wonder where everybody is.

Product-focused consultancies also fail to take account of the fact that most clients' working methods have altered dramatically in the last few years. It was not the design industry that invented the term downsizing. How many of your own clients now manage to leave work on time? I would guess that many of them are working late into the evening and over the weekend, running hard to stand still. How many of them have managed to keep human assistants rather than a personal computer, voicemail and mobile phone? How many of them have got the time to debate the finer points of design?

Market-focused consultancies, on the other hand, have recognized the pressures put on their clients, and are careful not to add to them. They keep ahead of new developments in their clients' marketplaces and – following Darwin's theory of evolution – they adapt and survive.

Here's a test. Are you a product-focused or a market-focused company? To find out, ask yourself the following simple questions:

1 In the last six months, have you formally discussed with each of your clients their general design needs, as opposed to project-specific needs?
2 Have you improved your core design offer in any way in the last 12 months in response to changing market or client needs (as opposed to any changes you might have made for the benefit of your own process or profitability)?
3 Do you currently have any specific plans to improve your core design offer in any way in the next 12 months?

If the answer to any of the questions is 'No', it is worth starting to do something about it now.

The Chartered Institute of Marketing defines the business of marketing as: 'The management process responsible for identifying, anticipating and satisfying customer requirements profitably.' I think that just about sums it up.

Where has your business come from?

Before you embark on the development of a new marketing programme, it is always useful to take a good look at what you have been doing in the past. Unless you are a brand new design consultancy about to launch yourself on the unsuspecting marketplace, you will already have been successful in gaining business. Where did that business come from? How did your clients find out about you in the first place? What made them decide to appoint you? How many stages did you have to go through before they became active clients?

It is useful to make a formal analysis of all the marketing activities you have undertaken in the past, and their results. Your analysis should include four key sections:

1 A full list of your clients for each of the past three years, together with the percentages of annual fee income they have provided.

This will tell you which clients' commissions are increasing or decreasing over the years and will alert you to potential problem areas, such as having one, or a very few, client companies accounting for a high proportion of your revenue. You should be aiming for a reasonably even spread of business to avoid the risks associated with relying too heavily on one or two individuals, bearing in mind that while XYZ client company might be the name on your list, your real client is one or more particular individuals in that company. If they move on, you might need to start again with that company.

CLIENT	*Year 1*	*Year 2*	*Year 3*
ABC Company	43%	24%	8%
DEF Company	17%	35%	47%
GHI Company	15%	16%	18%
JKL Company	14%	7%	11%
MNO Company	9%	–	12%
PQR Company	1%	4%	–
STU Company	1%	–	–
VWX Company	–	12%	3%
YZZ Company	–	2%	1%
	100%	100%	100%

2 Next, for each of these clients, identify how they got to know about you, and specifically the trigger that first got you talking to each other. If you are working for more than one client individual and his or her immediate colleagues, you will need to make the appropriate sub-divisions:

CLIENT	Trigger	
ABC Company	Project (i)	Recommendation from other client – DEF company
	Project (ii)	Recommendation from colleague at ABC company
DEF Company	Past client individual moved to company	
GHI Company	Cold approach from us – phone	
JKL Company	Cold approach from us – letter	
MNO Company	Phoned us after seeing press article	
PQR Company	Introduction from their PR company, working in our building	
STU Company	Our MD met them at conference	
VWX Company	Our Chairman's neighbour	
YZZ Company	Recommendation from other client – MNO company	

3 For each of these client companies, indicate the path of the sales process, so that you can track how you managed to convince them. How many competitive hurdles did you have to leap over?

CLIENT	Cold approach	Credentials	Proposal	Pitch
ABC Company (a)	–	yes	yes	–
(b)	–	yes	yes	yes
DEF Company	–	–	yes	–
GHI Company	yes	yes	yes	yes
JKL Company	yes	yes	yes	–
MNO Company	–	yes	yes	–
PQR Company	–	yes	yes	yes
STU Company	–	yes	yes	–
VWX Company	–	–	yes	–
YZZ Company	–	yes	yes	yes

4 Plot your marketing activities over the last three years, with their approximate cost and their known results in financial terms. Some companies find this difficult to do, as adequate records have not been kept. If this applies in your case, it is worth making an educated guess.

Three-year activity	Cost	Income	Profit
Cold approaches	£x	£y	£z
PR	£a	£b	£c
Advertising	£d	£e	£f
Networking	??	£d	£f

What this simple, four-part analysis will tell you is what has worked for you in the past, and what has not worked so well. For example, you might discover that your cold approach campaign has been more successful than you thought, or that meeting people at business events has provided the greatest part of your fee income. As a result, you will be able to build on the successful areas, and adjust or ignore those which failed. The analysis will also demonstrate the path you took to convert a potential client into an actual client: how many sessions did it take?

Activity 1

This first activity will identify the nature of your client business profile, the sources of their initial knowledge of your company, and the sales path required. It will also help you to start the process of assessing the results of your past marketing activities.

A Make a list of your clients over the last three years, and analyse the proportion of fee income each has provided.

B Identify how each of these clients got to know about you in the first place.

C Plot the route from first contact to formal commission: how many hoops did you have to jump through before working on that client's project?

D Analyse the effect of your marketing activities over the last three years. For each activity, look at the cost, followed by the financial results in fee income and profit. If you cannot assess profit on a project basis, use a general percentage based on your company's average profit on fee income.

2 WHERE ARE YOU GOING?

'When a man does not know which harbour he is aiming for, no wind is in the right direction.'
Seneca

- Company objectives
- Strategies for growth
- Marketing objectives

Company objectives

If you are not certain what you want to achieve with your company, you will never be able to develop good marketing objectives. Marketing is one – and only one – of the means by which you can pursue your overall commercial goals. If you do not know what you are pursuing, you will simply move in ever decreasing circles, getting nowhere.

The best objectives of any kind, regardless of the subject matter, are:

1 Challenging

Anita Roddick, founder of The Body Shop, says in her book *Body and Soul*: 'If you have a company with itsy-bitsy vision, you have an itsy-bitsy company.' Like her, think ambitiously; aim for distant harbours.

2 Realistic

If your desired goals are not achievable with your available resources, the result will be frustration and failure. If you lack the power to circumnavigate the world, aim for the next landfall, or stay within inland lakes. It would be better to cross a village pond successfully than to sink without trace in an ocean.

3 Specifically worded

Woolly statements like 'be seen as the most creative company in Europe', or 'increase our profitability' are not precise enough to be useful. What defines creativity? Exactly how much extra profit will be enough?

4 Clearly understood by all interested parties

Are you all steering in the same direction? If you want to test whether every member of your company is working towards the same set of objectives (and if they are not, then they are slowly but surely pulling your company apart by the seams), a good exercise is to ask everyone to write down their understanding of your business goal or mission. If there are any discrepancies, your company management should quickly communicate the key objectives to all staff. Failure in communication is never the fault of the recipient of the message, but of the sender.

5 Agreed by all interested parties

If you are heading for Polynesia and the rest of the company wants to go to Antarctica, you will be in trouble. The only way to get commitment is to include the key people in the decision process. Once the course has been agreed and charted, new arrivals will have to be content: if they don't like the destination, they always have the option of joining another ship instead.

6 Time-defined

All objectives should have a target date by which they should be achieved. Otherwise, you can keep on extending the limits indefinitely. If you have reached your destination within the planned timescale: good. If not: review the reasons, and make the necessary adjustments. It is worth looking at whether your objectives were realistic in the first place. It might be that the ocean you selected was too wide for your available resources.

7 Measurable

How will you know when you've got there? Like so many explorers, Christopher Columbus did not know exactly where he was when he reached his New World. How will you measure your own success or failure?

8 Frequently revised

Objectives should never be set in stone. Market changes, commercial opportunities and varying financial fortunes can either throw you off course, leave you in the doldrums, or give you a following wind. Learn to be flexible and to adjust your objectives whenever necessary.

Strategies for growth

Continuous growth is not, in itself, necessarily a desirable objective. Some companies reach an optimum operating size, where any increase would be disadvantageous. In such cases, the objective is to maintain the status quo, not to change it.

However, for the majority of companies, development through controlled growth is important for survival. Sometimes this is achieved through mergers with or acquisitions of other complementary companies. More often, it is achieved through sustained organic growth, and this is where marketing programmes can help.

There are four basic strategies for organic growth as shown in the chart.

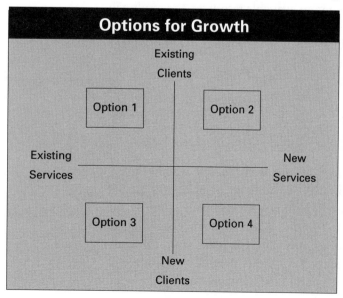

Options for Growth

Existing Clients

Option 1 Option 2

Existing Services New Services

Option 3 Option 4

New Clients

Option 1 Expand your business with existing clients, by selling them the fullest possible range of products or services from your current portfolio.

Option 2 Expand your business with existing clients, by developing new products or services for them.

Option 3 Start business with new clients, by selling them your current portfolio of products or services.

Option 4 Start business with new clients, by developing new products or services for them.

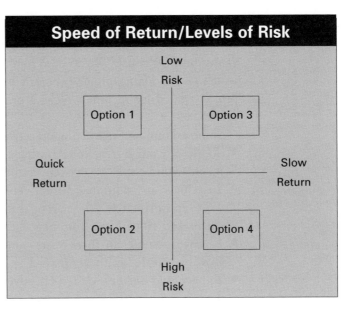

As the chart above shows, however, each of these has different associated speeds of return on your time and investment, and different levels of risk.

You will see that the order has changed from that in the previous chart. Most design companies choose the lower risk options of trying to sell existing products and services to both current and new clients. However, even though these routes might be both low on risk and swift on return, the key question each time has to be about the potential gain. For every organic growth strategy that you consider for your own company, you will need to weigh up the likely gain versus the likely risk; there is no universal answer.

Marketing objectives

Once you have decided where you want to go, you can work out how to get there. Only when you are clear about what you are trying to achieve with your marketing programme can the subsequent strategy and plan follow.

For example, are you trying to launch a new company or a new service to a new target market? If so, a big burst of activity followed by an ongoing reminder campaign might be appropriate. Or are you trying to increase your company's monthly fee income immediately from new clients? A marketing campaign which aims to raise awareness of your company's offer, combined with specific, highly targeted direct approaches to a few potential clients in a defined market sector in which you already have some expertise, would probably give you swifter results than approaches to potential clients in fresh market sectors.

For marketing objectives, financial goals should be always be expressed as fee income, and not as either turnover or profit. Why? As a business measurement, turnover is irrelevant; it simply expresses an amount of money passing through your bank account, in one day and out the next (or, if your cash flow isn't working properly, out one day and in several weeks later). In fact, there is a phrase which many design companies could usefully engrave over their doors: 'Turnover is vanity, profit is sanity.' We do need to remember, however, that profit is something which no marketing programme can produce on its own; it can simply deliver project-related fee income which, if properly managed, will produce the desired profit.

Some examples of marketing objectives might be:

- To increase our international business slowly, so that by the end of 2005 our fee income will be split 60 per cent domestic and 40 per cent overseas.
- To achieve an additional 30 per cent fee income every year for the next five years: approximately 20 per cent through increased expenditure from existing clients and 10 per cent from new clients.
- To have become, in three years' time, the principal design specialists in the growing private healthcare market.
- To have sold our new design effectiveness analysis programme to at least 15 of the top thousand client companies over the next six months.

Activity 2

This activity is designed to help you to work out what you want to achieve with your marketing programme.

A Define the overall business objectives for your company. Where do you want it to be in one, five and ten years' time?

Remember that your objectives should be:

- challenging but realistic
- specifically worded
- time-defined
- measurable.

Ultimately, of course, they should also be:

- clearly understood and agreed by all interested parties
- frequently revised.

B Decide whether you want a growth or a maintenance strategy over the next 12 months. If growth, is it to be through acquisition or organic? If organic, which of the four growth options outlined in this chapter would you choose, and in which order of priority, having weighed up the likely risk versus the likely gain?

C Define your marketing objectives for the next 12 months, based on your overall business objectives and growth strategy.

On marketing design services in general

LIZ LYDIATE: READER IN DESIGN MANAGEMENT, SURREY
INSTITUTE OF ART AND DESIGN AND DIRECTOR, DBA
PROFESSIONAL PRACTICE COURSE

- Because designers are terribly passionate about what they do, they can also be very stern critics of other people's work, and this can worry some clients.

I am going to start by making a plea for a more positive marketing stance. Throughout the design industry, there is a need for common standards and values. Designers need to stop undermining clients' confidence in design by showing more respect for it themselves; they can let the side down by being critical of other designers' work, and this leaves clients with the impression that dealing with design must somehow be difficult. When consultancies are trying to get a job, there is a great temptation to point out to the client everything that's wrong with the previous or existing work in order to say: 'You need us; we'll solve all of your problems and everything will be wonderful.' It would be better done in a more developmental way, through a sympathetic and intelligent discussion. Consultancies need to talk about the design the client has already got, how they got there, what is good about it and, of course, what can be improved: obviously the clients wouldn't be looking at other consultancies if they felt that there was nothing further to be done. However, there has been far too much root and branch design, of chucking everything out and starting again. There's a lot to be gained by putting more emphasis on exploring what's already there as a starting-point.

There is real value in specialization. Design consultancy has become more and more embedded in true business consultancy. It is now less self-contained within its own area, and involves a much more holistic approach. In order to provide that kind of consultancy, you have to know your client's business as well as your own, and obviously you can't do that across the board – it's just not possible. A lot of successful design companies have identified market sectors in which they like working, and to which they have a lot to contribute. They have developed a real expertise and knowledge about that sector, but they've also gone beyond that: they do positive things to become a part of that sector's world. They go to the events, they contribute to things, they look for ways of making themselves visible and relevant within their chosen client area. Design companies can sometimes make a start by making a key appointment of someone from a given sector. In this way, they can import a source of detailed knowledge and, more importantly, can use that source as seed corn to extend that knowledge throughout the company. It's not a case of 'Fred is our engineering expert', but 'Fred is an expert, and he's going to help the rest of us to become better at dealing with our engineering clients'.

A lot of marketing goes adrift by failing to match the offer with the actuality. When companies are marketing themselves, they make a number of statements – promises – about what life will be like as one of their clients. Those promises are expressed through brochures and credentials presentations and in all of the initial discussions with a new client. They form the main results areas, the client's expectations. They determine what the client thinks that he or she is going to get. As a consultancy, you can gain enormously by checking your delivery in a structured way against your initial offer. Are you delivering what you said you would? Are you still on target? That's the first stage. The next is, of course, to exceed what you said you would deliver. There is still a lot of discrepancy between what gets said at the courtship stage, and what actually happens, because there's not a defined structural link between the courtship conversation and the execution.

For long-term marketing, there is a lot of advantage to be gained from spreading throughout your client's organization knowledge and understanding of the design work that you are doing. What usually happens is that you are dealing with one key person, or a small group of people. Often, they do not know how important it is to tell their colleagues what's being done, how it works, how to look after it, what to expect from it. All too often, we see situations where excellent design work is no sooner received in an organization than it is spoilt – not by the commissioning client but by other people. You will have a business advantage if you make it part of your consultancy to say: 'Can we help you in teaching your colleagues about the work we are doing? Can we offer you any input or support?' You need to find ways of alerting the client to the fact that this aspect of the job has to be done in order for them to get full value from the design which they are buying.

Liz Lydiate has been responsible for the introduction of the BA Honours degree in Design Management at the Surrey Institute and for a pan-Institute programme of Professional Practice studies, which offers appropriate modules to students on all courses. For further information about its courses contact Surrey Institute of Art and Design, Falkner Road, Farnham, Surrey GU9 7DS, UK.

The Design Business Association (DBA) represents, supports and promotes the design consultancy sector. Among its many other activities, it runs a regular training programme, Professional Practice Stages I and II, of which Liz Lydiate is Course Director. For further information about membership, training and other activities contact DBA, 32 Saffron Hill, London EC1N 8FH, UK.

3 THE MARKETPLACE: CLIENTS' SELECTION CRITERIA

'Give me a firm place on which to stand, and I will move the earth.'
Archimedes, on the lever

- How clients buy design
- Rosters
- Why clients find buying design difficult
- How clients find out about design consultancies
- Why appoint a design consultancy at all?
- Decision-influencing criteria

How clients buy design

Before we start to think about developing a marketing programme, we need to understand how clients currently buy design consultancy services and what they are looking for. The first thing to appreciate is that the decision to spend money on design is almost always taken on an 'immediate needs' rather than a 'future wants' basis. In other words, the decision is both reactive and tactical, and very rarely made as part of a long-term strategic planning process. This statement might seem surprising, given the increasing recognition that design disciplines such as corporate identity, brand communications, retail environment design and product development have a significant commercial input to make to a client's business. However, all of these are bought on a needs basis, because of commercial problems and opportunities, or because of changes in a client company's circumstances such as mergers and acquisitions, or dramatic shifts in marketplaces. The fact that a design development programme might easily last for several years does not mean that the decision to do it was the result of ongoing financial planning. Clients will still see the expenditure as a one-off item, even though it might be spread over more than one fiscal year.

This is very different from the way in which, for example, advertising, public relations, building maintenance or human resources development expenditure is managed. For these items, regular annual expenditure budgets – however small – will be set, year after year, almost as a matter of course. They are so much a part of many client companies' business toolkits that they occupy a sort of default position: expenditure almost has to be prevented, rather than approved.

In contrast, there are very few client companies which allocate an overall budget for design at the beginning of their financial year. In fact, it is hard enough to get most clients to estimate the amount they have spent on design services in the past financial year, let alone plan budgets for the next. Design touches so many parts of their business activities, and is paid for by so many different departments, that auditing where the money has come from is often as difficult as measuring where it has gone to.

The second thing to appreciate is that clients do not, unlike design professionals, spend the majority of their working hours thinking about design. Although many clients would say that design is more stimulating to think about than, say, the viability of product price reductions or the implications of new legislative requirements, it is just one of the many business areas demanding their attention.

Thirdly, while more and more clients are actively establishing longer-term working relationships with design consultancies, it still remains the case that, within those relationships, design is bought on an ad-hoc basis. Very few design consultancies have managed to negotiate regular, pre-paid retainers with their clients. In practice, of course, there is very little benefit to a client in agreeing to such an arrangement. Why should they pay fees in advance to a design consultancy for an unknown requirement, when there is a large number of other design consultancies eager to receive a brief? On the other hand, clients are increasingly recognizing that formal rosters, or preferred suppliers' lists, are assets.

Rosters

Design rosters, as they are commonly called, are lists of the design companies approved by a certain client company or organization. They should more accurately be called Preferred Suppliers' Lists, as the term 'roster' suggests that design work is automatically allocated in turn to those on the list, which is not the case. They are lists of design companies which have been assessed by that client against quality, cost, delivery or other criteria.

Preferred suppliers lists are becoming increasingly popular in the larger client organizations. They allow clients to enjoy the benefit of long-term relationships with a limited number of design consultancies, with the added financial bonus of a pay-as-you-go system. A roster reduces the need for extensive research of the design supply market before the appointment is made, thus saving both time and effort. It will also ease the briefing procedure: a good, listed design consultancy will know the client's marketplace, products and customers almost as well as the client's own department. A roster is also, of course, an easy way for clients to deal with unwelcome approaches. The surprising thing is not how many clients have turned to the solution of working with formal rosters, but how few.

Design companies often express their frustration at the prevalence of preferred suppliers' lists, feeling that, because of the strict limits on numbers, the chances of being listed are slim. They say that when they contact a potential client with a roster, they are told – however nicely – that there is no point in continuing the conversation.

In fact, you stand as much chance of getting on to a particular roster as you would of working for that client if no formal roster existed. In terms of offering an open door to new business, the actual difference between client companies operating a formal roster system and those operating informal systems is precisely nil.

Clients have always worked with a small number of regular design suppliers: the only thing a roster does is to formalize the process. All good rosters are reviewed on a continuous basis, with a formal review and re-appointment or removal every year or 18 months, which gives an opportunity for additional or replacement design companies to be added at the same time. Where necessary, appointments will be made between reviews, when required for a specific purpose. No client company, for example, needing a multimedia specialist for a project would fail to appoint the best available company even if no such company were listed on their roster.

The alternative, less formal client system of working with a small number of design companies does not, despite appearances, offer a better chance of obtaining work. The design companies concerned often remain in place for many years, with companies only being removed if they make a complete disaster of a project, or added if an immediate need cannot be met by one of the usual suppliers.

Why clients find buying design difficult

Although there are some excellent and experienced clients who bring a whole new design management-based professionalism to the process of selecting and appointing design companies, they are relatively few in number. Most clients are not trained to buy and manage design services and, in practice, only rarely need to use the required skills in their everyday work. Financial directors, for example, usually trained as accountants. If they have not had to commission an annual report before, how do they know what is good or not from a design point of view, other than following their own personal preferences in taste?

In many cases, the purchasing process itself can be full of difficulties, usually brought about by the twin demons of lack of time and insufficient knowledge of the marketplace.

Shortened deadlines often mean that clients will choose to appoint a design company with whom they, or others in their company, have worked before, provided that the results were adequate and that the relationship is acceptable. In this scenario it is not necessary for a consultancy to have delivered exceptional results within an excellent relationship to be selected for a project. For a client with no time to waste it is easier to appoint a below-average consultancy rather than to spend time searching for a better one, briefing them in full, and running the considerable risks associated with using an untried resource. This is one of the few circumstances in which a design company can retain its clients without even trying.

And what about inadequate knowledge? Although a conservative estimate suggests that there are something in the region of 2000 design companies in the UK alone – and some would say that the figure is more like 4000 – most clients cannot name more than five design companies spontaneously. These five are usually a mixture of the consultancies the client has worked with and those which

Spontaneous Awareness of Design Consultancies	
	% of respondents
More than 20	1
15–20	3
10–15	11
5–10	45
Less than 5	38
None/don't know	2
Source: European Design Register	

appear frequently in articles in the trade or national press. A study carried out by the London-based European Design Register (EDR), which advises clients on the selection and management of design consultancies, demonstrates this clearly, as shown in the chart below. In their words: 'Despite the valiant effort of designers to stay top of mind amongst their potential clients, the awareness of individual consultancies is alarmingly poor.'

To compound the difficulty, it is not only the lack of knowledge of consultancies' names which causes problems for clients, it is also the lack of knowledge of what the different design companies offer, not helped by the poor communication skills of the consultancies themselves. This is what leads some clients to try to brief a corporate literature consultancy to look at branded packaging, a packaging specialist to quote on a retail interior project, or a retail specialist to design office interiors.

How clients find out about design consultancies

Good quality information about the design sector as a whole is thin on the ground. As has already been noted, clients source design company names in a variety of ways. They remember the companies which they have worked with in the past. They ask colleagues and friends for recommendations. They ask other business consultants, such as their PR and advertising agencies, or local or national government advisers. They will sometimes phone other clients whose design work they admire, and ask who did it. They use directories, if they can find any. They remember the names of consultancies they might have read about in the press, or who have contacted them directly in the past. They look in their filing cabinets for copies of brochures they have been sent.

Client Preferences for Compiling Short Lists	
	% mentions
Word of mouth	65
Past experience	60
Mailshots	10
Reference books	5
Direct approaches	5
Editorial	1
Advertising	1
Source: European Design Register	

Again, the EDR survey helps us to quantify the sources of information. As shown in the chart, clients were asked how they preferred to select design consultancies for their short lists.

The replies are revealing. The greatest level of trust, by far, is given to those companies which have been satisfactorily commissioned in the past, or which are believed to be good as a result of third-party recommendations and general reputation. We should not be too dismayed, however, at the relatively low percentages allocated to some of the more traditional marketing levers such as direct approaches, editorial and advertising. Think about how you and your colleagues buy products and services for your own business. Having made the decision to select a certain supplier, most of us would be unable to identify with absolute confidence what it was that influenced our choice; it is usually a combination of things. Moreover, none of us likes to think that we can be 'sold' to, either directly or indirectly; we prefer to believe that we make our own informed choices. Nevertheless, word of mouth is probably the most powerful marketing tool we possess, and it isn't as cheap as it might at first appear. It takes years to build up a good reputation but, as in so many fields, you are only as good as your last job. This subject will be explored in greater detail in Chapter 12.

Why appoint a design consultancy at all?

The commercial design supply business is still young enough to need a helping hand in the form of generic promotion. In all markets, the first job to be done is to convince people that they need the item or service in question: selection between brands comes later. Think of faxes, automatic dishwashers, independent financial advisers, fast food outlets. Until we have convinced ourselves that we need something, the relative merits of one company or brand over another are irrelevant. It is only when substantial numbers of people have convinced themselves that they need something that markets begin to mature.

At present, not all clients know that they need design. To adapt the old saying: some clients know they need it some of the time, some clients even know they need it all of the time. However, it will take some time before we reach a point when all of the clients believe that they need it all of the time. If we start from the assumption that decisions will be made on a 'which do I need?' basis, rather than a 'do I need it at all?' basis, we will fail to connect.

So, how can we convince potential clients that design works? Not by just telling them, that's for sure. We need to persuade them, to show them actively that design in all of its many forms is an essential business tool. We need to demonstrate that, when it is properly managed, design brings about beneficial change to a company, organization, product or brand. We need to explain that design should be seen as an investment, not a cost, and that it will contribute to commercial effectiveness.

Who should take on this task? Some of the industry bodies for design across the world are already starting to do a great deal of work in this area, whether those bodies are government funded or financed only by membership subscriptions. However, there is still a generic job to be done by every single person working in design. We must all work together as an industry to understand and promote design effectiveness overall, as well as promoting the relative merits of our own particular companies. We need to position design itself in a more meaningful way: it should not be seen as a luxury item ('it would be an advantage to have it, but we don't really need it') but as an essential part of the commercial machinery ('We could not operate without it').

To compound the difficulties, out of the numbers of those clients who know they need design, not all know that they need commercial design consultancy services. There are plenty of other places from which a client can buy design advice. Advertising, direct marketing and sales promotion agencies offer corporate identity, sales literature and packaging design, as do printers and packaging converters. Shopfitters and architects offer retail and other interiors. The industrial design sector is slightly better protected than its counterparts in graphics and interiors but, whereas the long-term commercial benefits of corporate, brand or retail interior design are beginning to be more widely accepted right across the developed world, many manufacturers are still reluctant to spend serious money on product design, a particularly ironic situation given that it is industrial design effectiveness which is the best documented. Design companies also need to convince clients of the advantages of external skills over those available to a client in-house. As has been noted before, there are very many excellent in-house design units, and independent design companies ignore them at their peril.

The chain of thought in the purchase process is, therefore, longer than many design consultancies realize. To reach the point when a client starts to get in touch with a design consultancy – or to actively listen to approaches – the chain follows a winding path, and can be snapped at any point at a weak link. It goes:

Stage 1   I have a business problem or an opportunity. What tools are available to me to help me?

Stage 2   Of the many tools which I have identified, I believe that design can contribute to helping me to achieve my objectives. Where can I get some from?

Stage 3   Of the sources of design services open to me, I believe that an independent, external consultancy will be the best choice. How can I find out who offers what I need?

Only now does the thought process reach the point where most design consultancies think that it starts, the moment at which the whole independent design consultancy sector enters the equation. The next inevitable stages will be:

Stage 4   Of the design consultancies I know, or have been able to find out about, which of them shall I shortlist to prepare proposals on which I can base my final decision?

Stage 5   Of the shortlisted candidates, which one has convinced me that it is the right one for my business problem or opportunity?

The last two stages lead to the crunch question in any marketing strategy: why should an individual person from a particular company in a certain business sector choose you instead of one of your competitors?

Decision-influencing criteria

Every project from every individual in every client company will be different. Different criteria will therefore apply to the selection of the right design consultancy for that project. However, there are certain common factors which determine whether a client will (a) find your company's offer attractive enough to appoint you in the first place and (b) appoint you again once he or she has worked with you and experienced your offer in practice. There are 12 main decision-influencing criteria.

Clients' decision-influencing criteria

1   Quality of product
2   Commercial awareness
3   Value for money
4   Level of service
5   Problem-solving ability
6   Project management ability
7   Business track record
8   Expertise in a design discipline
9   Expertise in a specific market
10 Appropriate size for the project
11 Location
12 People chemistry

The final decision will be based, of course, on that heady cocktail of perception and reality. Before a client has experienced working with you, perception is stronger than reality. This perception comes from statements made by you (for example in letters, brochures, telephone calls and meetings) and from statements made by their colleagues, friends, other business advisers and the media – in other words from a collection of opinion-formers. The reality is based on the client's limited observation of what you actually do and how you behave during the period before appointment, as opposed to what you say.

Once a client has worked with you the balance changes, and reality forms the greater part of the mix. However, never underestimate the continuing power of word-of-mouth to affect your business for the better or for the worse, even when pitted against experience. We all know that reality lags far behind perception: an average company or product or service with a great historical reputation will be in a much stronger position than an excellent one with a poor historical reputation. We forgive companies we admire if they transgress, and we continue to criticize detested companies even when they provide excellent results for us. Our brains seem to refuse to acknowledge what our eyes and ears are telling us.

Let's take a look at the 12 decision-influencing criteria in detail.

1 Quality of product

We can break quality down into three categories: acceptable, good and best. As far as clients are concerned, an acceptable design product is one which achieves the required results; it is appropriate for the task and it fulfils the objectives set for it, regardless of whether the design involves an exciting new innovation or a simple adjustment to an existing product. A good design product is appropriate for the task, fulfils its objectives and is also well received within the client's own organization; praise (or otherwise) from colleagues and employers will naturally affect the client's view of the final design. However, the very best design products are those which are appropriate for the task, fulfil their objectives, are well received and, in addition, have that little bit extra, that touch of creativity. They are 'entirely fit for the purpose, plus a bit'.

When asked, clients will almost always place the need for creative excellence at the top of their lists. In a way, this is a fairly obvious requirement, as it is the one thing which can not usually be provided adequately from their own resources. Even the many companies which have in-house design departments feel – often wrongly – that they have to place more challenging design projects with external suppliers.

On the other hand, clients claim that they do not always get enough creativity, which they equate with originality, saying that they are shown recycled and derivative ideas: 'If I am shown another annual report with a bit of tracing paper in it/see-through escalator in an atrium/stainless steel minimalist kitchen object/etc,' they say, 'I shall scream.'

This presents a dilemma for design consultancies, who have occasionally been known to take the view that some of their clients would not recognize a truly original creative idea if it bit them on the ankle. How, then, can you fulfil your clients' stated needs for creativity with their understandable nervousness in approving boundary-bending work? It is a question of managing your client's expectations, of acclimatization. A cynic might advise you to show your creative idea at the same time as another idea which is twice as daring, twice as outrageous; the recommended design then pales into acceptable normality in comparison. A design management consultant, however, would advise you to demonstrate that the end-user or the consumer of the product or service in question would find the proposed idea perfectly acceptable, either because the visual vocabulary is familiar to that consumer group, or because you have tested the concept among them. The important word here is demonstrate – not tell. You will need to spend time, money or both on desk or field research in order to gather the evidence you need.

2 Commercial awareness

However creative and original your consultancy's work, you will only convince a client of your worth if you add a demonstration of your sound commercial acuity. The more you can do to link the words 'design' and 'effective' the better; there is no reason whatsoever why design which looks good should not also be good (and vice versa). You need to prove that you know that design has one fundamental purpose: to bring about commercial results for a client's business.

The UK Design Business Association (DBA) has pioneered the introduction of the Design Effectiveness Awards, which are open to design companies throughout the world, both members and non-members. The entries to these awards have contributed a great deal to the industry's knowledge of how the design element of a product or service works once it joins the marketplace. To many design advisers' regret, the case studies are not published in full in book form, although the awards summary contains some useful insights.

You will also need a detailed knowledge of how your own design discipline works in general, and also how it works in a particular market sector. For example, in retail, issues like traffic flow and security have certain universal principles, but they will require different design solutions in, say, an up-market travel goods shop as opposed to a city centre multi-storey music and video store. The financial return on investment in a new pack design for a leading petfood brand will follow a different pattern from that on investment in a special seasonal bubble bath. The cost of design development for a new pocket calculator is insignificant when compared with the cost of that for a new motorbike, but one is likely to contribute more quickly to increased revenue for its client than the other.

3 Value for money

We all know that value for money is independent from absolute price. We are happy to pay a very low price for a pair of plastic shoes to wear on holiday, and a very high price for a pair of high-tech walking boots or sports shoes. Here, the decision is performance- and benefit-related; we believe that either price point gives us good value for money. However, it is not always that simple. We might pay a certain amount for a pair of leather fashion shoes from a high street chain store, or five or six times that amount for a similar pair of leather fashion shoes with a couturier label. Why? Because it makes us feel good, because our choice of shoes says something about us. The purchase still provides us with value for money.

Consciously or unconsciously, clients will also select design companies on a combination of performance and aspiration; just as with shoes, either can provide perceived value for money. At the initial appointment stage, it is almost impossible for potential clients to make an accurate assessment. Before receiving a cost estimate from you, they will base their decision on perceived value for money, on your answers to their questions about the costs of projects you might show them as case studies, and on their perception of the way you run your business. When they visit your premises, for example, they will want to see evidence of success, but not excess. After receiving your cost estimate, they will compare it with estimates from your competitors, which in itself causes difficulties: very rarely are they comparing apples with apples.

Of course, after working with you, your clients will be able to state quite clearly whether you have provided value for money or not: the evaluation will always depend on the final quality of the product, plus the level of service you have given.

4 Level of service

Service is not the same as being servile. True service is about providing the best possible advice and the best possible implementation practices to our clients. There are two aspects to good service: the intellectual and the emotional. Intellectually, clients will assess your service levels on measurable, identifiable actions. Emotionally, they will assess your level of service on less tangible issues. There is more on actual levels of service in Chapter 12.

Start as you mean to go on, and treat every potential client as though they were your most cherished actual client. Phone when you say you will, confirm everything in writing, and make sure that if they visit your premises they are welcomed by name. Whenever you show work done for another client, mention any significant aspects of the project which were based on good service.

5 Problem-solving ability

Can you demonstrate that you add value to design by thinking about the issues around the brief as well as the issues in it? If you call yourself a consultancy, provide a consultancy service. Using your experience, spend time working out what a client might really need, as well as what they have said they want. Briefing a design consultancy is very difficult to do well; it is easy to spot what is there, but not what has been left out.

6 Project management ability

If you cannot demonstrate your project management skills to potential clients before you are appointed, there is little hope of your doing so afterwards. Are all of your communications accurate? A badly written brochure, mailshot or letter will be a deterrent. Do you meet your promises? Do you act promptly? When showing case study work, do you mention the project management skills which contributed to its success? It is not a question of whether or not you have dedicated project managers or client liaison people in your company; the task of project management needs to be done properly in either case.

Of course, all of your work for actual clients must be on time or before, on budget or lower, and always on brief, even if you decide to go that extra mile and present your client with some additional, alternative ways of looking at the subject.

7 Business track record

A potential client will look at how long you've been in business and your performance over that time, and will assess your commercial viability. To have a design company close in the middle of a project causes nothing but complications. Your client list will also be scrutinized; have you worked for major companies? If so, most potential clients will take comfort from that fact. There is always a risk associated with appointing an untried design company, no matter how established that company might be. If the project should go wrong for any reason, clients will be faced with criticism from within their own organizations. The success or failure of a design project can also affect their career development. In the case of failure, one line of defence is that X, Y and Z client companies – all well respected in their fields – have also commissioned you to do design work. Can they all be wrong?

8 Expertise in a design discipline

If you have never designed an annual report, motorbike, restaurant, glass jar or widget before, which brave client will be the first to let you try? Who is going to pay for the inevitable learning curve? Increasingly, design consultancies are specializing in one discipline, and often in one aspect of that discipline, especially in the crowded and competitive area of graphics. For example, there are consultancies which only work on structural packaging, or only on annual reports. If you want to break into a new discipline in which you have no previous experience, you will have to either design and field trial something in your own time and with your own funds, or recruit or sub-contract to a specialist in that discipline.

9 Expertise in a specific market

This is one of those double-edged swords. From time to time, clients believe that their own market is unique, and that only those people who really understand it will be able to solve its problems and meet its opportunities. To an extent, that is correct; if a client commissions someone who already knows about a market, they will save on the amount of time needed for briefing and familiarization, and on the false starts which can dog the early stages of a design project. On the other hand, they might inherit blinkered thinking. In addition, unless you have decided to specialize in, say, design for the legal profession or marine engineers and nothing else, there will always be the concern about a design consultancy working for two competitive clients. On the whole, though, potential clients are reassured if a design company knows something about an actual or a related market: it is up to you to convince them that your knowledge is sufficient.

10 Appropriate size for the project

Clients often feel, rightly or wrongly, that a large project will swamp a small design consultancy, and that a small project will not get the attention it deserves in a large company. If they are to be the largest client for any one design company, they feel that they will never get unbiased advice, since the design company's financial future depends on their commissions. Conversely, if they do not provide a significant part of a design company's income, they feel that their work will be done by junior, inexperienced staff. So far, so obvious. There are, however, more subtle forces at work. Some clients feel that the way in which a large consultancy handles an apparently unappealing, small project is a fair indication of its attitude to business overall, and will occasionally try out a design company in this way without indicating their future plans. Other clients know that a small company can quickly gear up to manage a larger than usual project, and are willing to support that route if there are other benefits to be had from using their design, their management expertise or their experience of the market sector.

11 Location

For major projects involving unique skills or specific design discipline or market sector expertise, the distance between the client and the design consultancy locations is irrelevant. If this were not the case, all design would be supplied on a local basis. For minor projects, where the additional time and costs associated with the travelling (for either party) are out of proportion either to the total budget or to the long-term significance of the project itself, a near location becomes more attractive. Clients are still drawn to major cities for top-quality design. They feel that is where the best design companies are based, and where the most talented staff will want to work. Conversely, design companies which are based outside such cities should remember that they will be very attractive to local clients, and that with more and more companies decentralizing, there are many large clients with needs to be met just sitting on their doorsteps. You should never apologize for your location, but focus instead on the benefits of working with your particular company. If challenged, assure potential clients from outside your immediate area that the distance is not a problem.

12 People chemistry

Even if everything else points to your appointment, if the potential client does not like you or your colleagues, you will not be selected. In a way, there's not much you can do if this situation occurs, but it is worth making sure that more than one person meets potential clients in order to reduce the risk. For existing clients, a weather eye should be kept on all of your ongoing projects and relationships. If there are any problems, change the team and keep the client.

Activity 3

This activity is designed to encourage you to think about design from a client's point of view, and then to find out whether or not you were right.

A Select three of your current client individuals. For each of them, try to work out what they are likely to want from design consultancy services in general – not just from you and your company – and write it down, listing the decision-influencing criteria in priority order. You can use the 12-point checklist as a prompt, but there will certainly be other needs which are specific to each individual or to their company.

B Make time to ask each of those clients about their design-buying criteria, and compare their answers with the results of your session. Most clients, by the way, are willing to have their opinions sought and can be very helpful with their answers, particularly if you explain that you are developing ways to improve your offer. If this exercise is done regularly, it will be seen as an integral part of your customer care programme.

4 WHAT ARE YOU? HOW TO ESTABLISH YOUR POSITIONING

'Know thyself.'
Inscription over door in temple at Delphi

- Products and positions
- Competitive mapping
- Strengths and weaknesses
- Generalism versus specialism
- Current and desired positioning

Products and positions

If you cannot clearly explain to yourself what you are, what you do, who you do it for and how you do it, how can you hope to explain it to other people? A positioning statement describes your core activity and is a useful way to start the development of your marketing programme. Once you have defined your basic product – to be regularly improved, as we have already seen, in line with changing market needs – you can work out exactly who might want it, why they might bother appointing you instead of anyone else, and how they will be able to find out about you in the first place.

Your positioning in your chosen marketplace will depend partly on what other people think of you and your work in relation to what your competitors are offering, and partly on the way you choose to present yourself to the outside world.

One example of the strength of positioning can be seen in the supermarket business. One chain might position itself as an out-of-town, pile-it-high, budget store. Another might decide to present itself as the reliable, quality, family store. A third might decide to place itself firmly as the place to get more upmarket, unusual foods. They will all sell tea, coffee, milk and sugar, and they will all have to invest in property, fixtures and fittings, and staff. The difference between them lies in which segment of the market they have decided to claim as their own high ground. Their products, prices, promotional campaigns and places of operation (the traditional 'Four Ps' of the marketing mix) will be selected as a result of that decision, not before. None of these market positions is inherently better than the others: they are all just consciously different.

It is also possible for one product, company or brand to be positioned in different ways to more than one target market. A shampoo might be positioned as a baby product in one country, and a natural, herbal adult product in another: the formulation is identical in each case, but the positioning differs. In the design world, sole designers might decide to present themselves to direct clients as independent strategic design consultants, and to design groups as freelancers. The person and their abilities remain the same; it is the positioning which differs.

Competitive mapping

In order to define your current positioning, you will need to be clear about your competitors. Who are they? What do they do? How do they do it?

Once you start to look critically at your competitors, you might discover that they are not as numerous as you had feared. The fact that there may be around 2000 design companies working in the UK does not mean that each company has 1999 competitors. Even within one, narrow design discipline, not all companies are competitive. For example, a commercial interior design company specializing in boardrooms and office suites for directors might not be directly competitive with one working on large-scale commercial offices.

It can be helpful to produce a map or grid of other design companies which you consider to be hot, warm and cool competitors. Hot competitors are those design consultancies or other suppliers with whom your existing clients are currently working, and those to whom your clients might turn if they decided not to work with you any longer. They will be the ones you find yourself regularly pitching against for work: if you don't know who they are, ask. They are also likely to be consultancies which not only offer the same precise discipline as you, but which are similar to you in size, culture and location. In practice, most design companies have no more than four or five truly hot competitors. These are the ones to watch like a hawk. You should almost be able to write their business plans for them.

Warm competitors are those design consultancies or other suppliers which offer the same kind of work, but which in your judgement, and for whatever reason, do not fall into quite the same bracket as you. These might well be the largest group, and they are the ones to keep under constant low-level surveillance.

Cool competitors are those companies or other suppliers which could offer similar services, but do not at present. They are ones to keep an eye on from a distance. Depending on your precise discipline, they could be very numerous, or very few.

The term 'other suppliers' has been used. Not all of your competitors will be design consultancies. For example, advertising agencies, sales promotion and direct marketing companies, printers and packaging converters can all provide many elements of corporate and brand design. Some high street copy shops employ graphic designers and produce acceptable brochures and stationery ranges, at a fraction of the cost and time taken by consultancies. Architects can, and do, offer a wide selection of interior design skills. In-house design departments get involved right across the board, but particularly in product or industrial design. You will need to decide for yourself which category they fit into – hot, warm or cool; it will depend both on the sector you are working in and the quality of the in-house unit. Some will be red hot competitors, others decidedly lukewarm.

One way to plot the competitive profile is through the simple use of columns:

HOT	WARM	COOL
YZZ	GHI	DEF
JKL	VWX	STU
MNO		PQR
		ABC

A more sophisticated way is to select several dimensions on which comparisons could be made, and map the identified companies accordingly. For example:

EQUIVALENT CREATIVITY

VWX YZZ STU   PQR JKL ABC MNO

HOT . . . . COOL

EQUALLY GOOD CLIENT LIST

MNO YZZ ABC   VWX JKL PQR STU

HOT . . . . COOL

STRONG STRATEGIC ABILITY

YZZ JKL MNO   ABC DEF GHI STU MNO

HOT . . . . COOL

Strengths and weaknesses

Having identified the opposition, you can now work out your own strengths and weaknesses in relation to them. First, get together a group of people from your company with a large piece of paper divided into two sections marked strengths and weaknesses. Try to get as much written down as possible in true brainstorming style – without comment or criticism – and edit it later with the help of one or two key colleagues. The important thing is to encourage everyone to be as honest as possible about your weaknesses, but justifiably proud of your strengths. Secondly, ask your clients. You will find some additional insights creeping into your thinking; they are able to view your company both as an informed outsider and as someone with knowledge of other design companies.

If you want to take it further, you can turn it into a full SWOT analysis (Strengths, Weaknesses, Opportunities and Threats) as in the chart below.

As an example, the chart overleaf shows a very simple SWOT analysis based on the issue of marketing the Western European design community as a whole to the rest of the world. You will see that a strength can also be a weakness if looked at from a different angle, that strengths can suggest opportunities, that weaknesses can lead to potential threats, and that opportunities and threats can be interchangeable.

SWOT Analysis

STRENGTHS	WEAKNESSES
What can we do?	What can we not do?
What are we good at?	What do we do badly?
What assets do we have?	What assets do we lack?
OPPORTUNITIES	THREATS
What might increase	What might get in the
our business potential?	way of our progress?

European Design Consultancies	
STRENGTHS	**WEAKNESSES**
Expertise	Poor non-European languages ability
Experience	Small companies/few resources
Small companies/personal service	
Good reputation worldwide	
OPPORTUNITIES	**THREATS**
Other markets	Other non-design consultancy
● Japan and Far East	suppliers to our clients
● Australia	In-house client departments/DIY
● Middle East	Local design consultancies (location)
● Eastern Europe	Failure to keep pace with/afford
● USA	technological developments
New services	Difficult client economy
● design management	Other countries speak our languages
consultancy	
Technological developments	

Generalism versus specialism

Once you have examined your own strengths and weaknesses, and explored the way in which you are currently perceived, either by choice (you've worked hard at establishing that perception) or by default (others have decided it for you), you can consider whether you should be a specialist or a generalist, and to what extent.

Specialism can be an advantage. The UK financial and management consultants Willott Kingston Smith stated in their February 1996 edition of their regular publication *Marketing Monitor:* 'Whilst the overall results for the [design] sector continue to be uncertain, we are aware of several consultancies which are experiencing buoyant business. In general terms, these would be the ones with a particular niche, or who have added value to their basic service.'

To a large extent, however, your decision on how specialist or generalist to be will also depend on the prevailing conditions of the precise market in which you are working. In geographical markets in which the commercial design sector is newly established – such as some Eastern European countries – a generalist approach is normal. Consultancies offer everything from the design of industrial manufacturing components, to the creation of restaurant interiors and their menus. However, in more mature markets, such as Western Europe and North America, only the very largest design groups can realistically offer a department store service to their clients. Most will offer only one design discipline. Equally, in business sectors where the use of design as a business tool is commonplace – such as FMCG (fast moving consumer goods) packaging, corporate communications and consumer product manufacturing – there is an increasing tendency towards highly specialist services. Generally speaking, developed geographical markets and design-hungry business sectors both tend to spawn large numbers of competitive design consultancies. The more competitive the market, the greater the need for specialism.

However, we have to ask ourselves how specialist is specialist? Do you supply one particular kind of design service? Or do you concentrate on one client business sector? Or do you do both, for example offering only annual reports to financial services organizations and no one else? There are design companies which have chosen to offer nothing but interior design for the custom-built yachts sector, or packaging for number two brands, or paper engineering, or television graphics, or literature for charities. They have all identified markets where there is a genuine need for specialist knowledge, and a sufficiently large market to provide enough work. If you are the only company in the world who can do something which enough clients want, you are in an enviable position.

The trouble with spotting a gap in the market is that you swiftly have to follow your exclamation of 'Eureka!' with the tough question: 'But is there a market in the gap?' The reason some design disciplines are so crowded is that there is a continuous need for the services which that discipline provides. An empty field might mean that everyone else has decided not to enter for very good reasons. You will need to research each apparent gap carefully to be confident that what seems like a straight road to commercial success does not turn out to be a dead-end alley.

Clearly, a degree of specialism can help with your marketing task. It is always much easier to gain a reputation for a particular expertise than for a general ability. Your offer will also be more credible, especially if your company is compact in numbers: how can you possibly be good at everything? In practice, it is wise for most design companies to remain within one ring-fenced area, offering a complementary range of services to a limited number of client business sectors.

Current and desired positioning

A good way to work out your current positioning is to describe yourself as though to a new solicitor or accountant who has started working for you, and who has asked you about your work. In other words, to someone who is rather like a client: intelligent, but lacking in detailed knowledge about you. If you discover that you are describing yourself as 'one of the many companies which does x, y or z', then your positioning may be too general, and it has probably been gained by default, rather than by choice.

Based on the work you have done on mapping your competitors, working out your absolute and relative strengths and weaknesses and deciding on your likely specialist versus more generalist approach, you can decide whether you want to alter your positioning in any way for the future.

The following are all examples of positioning statements for design companies:

- We design motorbikes: we are the only company in the world which can combine the engineering advantage of an advanced engine with the ergonomic needs of the rider.
- We specialize in design for international brands: we offer packaging (structural

and graphic), brand identities, and brand sales support materials (literature, point-of-sale etc).

- We design cost-effective annual and interim annual reports and accounts for charities and other not-for-profit organizations.
- Our expertise is in the design of innovative component parts for the transport and aerospace industries.
- We design and produce business-to-business communications materials.
- We are the design experts of the European franchise retail market: we provide interiors, shop front and signage programmes, literature, packaging, point-of-sale.
- We specialize in the design of environmentally-balanced and eco-friendly office interiors: we offer design and build, with affiliated architectural and landscaping expertise when required.

Activity 4

This activity will help you to establish your current positioning in the marketplace, and to start to define a future workable positioning.

A Map out your competition into hot, warm and cool sections. First, do it in simple columns, and then have a go at plotting them against several dimensions relevant to your business. See if any score consistently highly: these will be your hottest competitors.

B Do an analysis of your own strengths and weaknesses, following the SWOT (Strengths, Weaknesses, Opportunities and Threats) model if you feel that it is useful. As a minimum, set out your strengths and weaknesses in two columns.

C Do the same analysis on each of your main competitors as well.

D Think about which areas of specialism might prove fertile for you. You will, of course, have to follow this up with detailed research on any likely contenders. Consider:
- what you do, or could, offer
- what your real expertise is
- client market sectors in which you have experience.

E Define your company's current positioning in your marketplace (default or planned).

F Think about what you would like your company's positioning to be:
- in five years' time
- in ten years' time.

On the principles of marketing design services abroad

RICHARD WATSON: EUROPEAN DESIGN REGISTER

- In many countries, for example Germany, Italy and Thailand, design work is still being done predominantly by advertising agencies. The good news is that they are not very good at it. The bad news is that clients haven't yet realized this.

How do you market yourself successfully abroad? It can be easier than selling your services to your domestic market if you have the right resources. Technology obviously makes things a lot easier, with clients and design companies linked electronically for the swift exchange of ideas and material.

Serious contenders – and some of the more successful design companies gain over 70 per cent of their work from overseas clients – tend to have a mixture of foreign nationals working for them. The benefit is more to do with perception and attitude than a need for language diversity. The reality is that most client companies working across a global market have people who speak English as an international business language, and who are themselves often not nationals of the country in which the company is based.

If you are working in a very competitive market such as packaging, a good model is to have a local agent to do the new business meetings, and to have the work done at home. If you are a real specialist in your field, and know that there are only a few companies in the world who can do what you do, it is much more possible to export directly.

It is reasonably easy to source contact details for potential clients overseas. Published lists, directories and databases exist for most countries. The tricky bit is to identify which company owns which brands; it can sometimes take a long time. The level of seniority of the potential client varies from country to country, with marketing directors in France or Germany being responsible for the sorts of projects managed by, say, a brand manager in the UK. You also have to think about regional and territorial differences in certain countries. For example, companies in Hamburg prefer to deal with other companies from Hamburg; a design company from Frankfurt could have almost the same difficulties getting through to them as one from London. The same situation applies in Spain, where a client in Barcelona might simply refuse to employ a design company from Madrid.

The new markets at present are not in Western Europe or America but in Asia (especially China and Thailand), the Pacific Rim, India and Pakistan, and the Commonwealth Independent States. There is a boom in these countries both in terms of the need for professional design services and in terms of the volume of work. The problem is that they are 20 years behind Europe; finding a brief is easy, finding the budget is not.

Design companies sometimes think that it's so tough in their own country that they try to seek work overseas without having worked out a proper marketing strategy. As a result, they tend to end up with the same problems; the only difference is that it costs a lot more. It is so important to get your positioning sorted out first. Think of your company as a brand, and think long term: no brands were built overnight.

The European Design Register (EDR) advises clients on the selection and management of UK, European and worldwide design consultancies. Its expertise covers corporate identity, corporate literature, retail and interior design, branding and packaging, and product design. For further information, contact EDR, 11–12 Tottenham Mews, London W1P 9PJ, UK.

5 WHO WANTS YOU? HOW TO DECIDE ON YOUR TARGET MARKETS

'To accomplish good design, you need a good client.'
Le Corbusier

- Vertical and horizontal sectoring
- Clients, middlemen and decision-making
- Geographical limits
- Demographic targeting
- Psychographic targeting

Vertical and horizontal sectoring

In strategic planning for marketing, it is impossible to separate a desired target market from a deliverable product and its positioning. Within the subject area of generalism and specialism in Chapter 4, we found that only very few design groups could realistically offer a wide range of design disciplines and services to an equally wide range of business sectors. For example, with sufficient resources it is perfectly possible for a large consultancy to be experts in, say, the design of high-speed trains and the design of newspaper mastheads. Within a narrower field, the larger graphics companies can cover both corporate and brand work, although the target markets are very different. This is almost always achieved by dividing the company resources into two or more apparent divisions, which enjoy the use of common administrative functions. In this way, the company is seen to offer two excellent specialisms instead of one average generalism.

For the majority of design consultancies, however, it is advisable to offer either a complementary range of services to a fairly narrow band of client sectors (vertical sectoring) or a specific service to a wide band (horizontal sectoring). With vertical sectoring, your expertise lies in the provision of several linked services to one (or a very few) business areas. With horizontal sectoring, you are providing expertise in one particular skill to as many business sectors as possible. A few simple examples of each are shown in the charts overleaf.

Obviously, the examples given are for demonstration purposes, and are therefore somewhat simplistic. In practice, if you are going to employ the strategy of vertical sectoring, it is wise to select three or four business sectors and run parallel, or multi-track, promotional programmes against each of them. This will make sure that you cover the market more thoroughly and avoid the risk of attaching your fortunes to the coat tails of one sector alone. Many design companies which chose to concentrate on retail in the early 1990s were badly wounded during the global

Vertical Sectoring		
DESIGN DISCIPLINE	TARGET SECTOR	PRODUCT AND POSITIONING
Interior design	Retail clients	The design and implementation of stores, staff restaurants, receptions, offices, training rooms and other operational areas, with the provision via associates of the additional services of landscaping, architecture and communication graphics.
Industrial design	Leisure transport	The design and prototype of cars, motorbikes, watercraft and small aircraft, their component parts and related manufacturing process systems and tools, with the provision via associates of the additional services of brand identity and communication literature.
Graphic design	FMCG (fast moving consumer goods) companies	The design and implementation of corporate identity and communications, brand identity, packaging and sales support literature, and human resources materials, with provision via associates of the additional services of multimedia and video communications, and interior and industrial design.

Horizontal Sectoring		
DESIGN DISCIPLINE	TARGET SECTOR	PRODUCT AND POSITIONING
Interior design	Top UK 1000 companies	The design of reception areas, boardrooms, directors' offices, directors' dining-rooms, corporate flats.
Industrial design	Consumer goods manufacturers	The design, style and prototype of electrical consumer products.
Graphic design	European plcs	The design and production of printed human resources materials: recruitment literature, information brochures, training manuals, conference materials, forms and documentation systems.

recession, which hit the high street retail trade particularly badly.

Equally, if you are going to apply horizontal sectoring principles, you need to make sure that your chosen area of product expertise has a future life. For example, consultancies which used to specialize in printed catalogue design and production are rapidly having to acquire interactive multimedia skills.

Clients, middlemen and decision-making

Most design is bought directly by commissioning clients, who will source, select, brief and pay you. The resulting relationship – good or bad – is entirely straightforward.

A small proportion of design, however, is bought by third parties or middlemen who are acting on behalf of their own clients. Middlemen do not often commission design in product and interior design, but they are fairly common in the graphics world, where they would include management consultants, PR companies and advertising agencies. They will, of course, add a percentage mark-up to your invoices before billing their clients, as a fee for their consultancy time and to cover the potential risk to their cash flow. They will always, therefore, look for the best possible work at the keenest prices: the results will reflect on their own professionalism, but they need to be able to add their percentage without sending the total project figure to the stars.

Increasingly, with the growth of design management as a discipline, a middleman client might be someone with a great deal of experience in buying design. It is quite possible to offer design as a product without employing any designers: one or two consultancies already work in this way, by putting together design individuals and companies on an ad hoc basis as a kind of virtual company. Most design management consultants prefer not to offer design services themselves, but to remain as advisers to the client company. They will, of course, often be involved in the selection and appointment of a suitable design supplier, and will occasionally manage or oversee the whole project.

Within the purchase process, the commissioning client – whether direct or third party – is the decision-maker. However, as shown in the chart below, he or she will be strongly influenced by a number of other parties. These, as we have seen earlier in Chapter 3, can include:

- colleagues from the same company
- appointed consultants, such as advertising agencies and PR or management consultants
- friends working in similar fields
- past colleagues from other companies
- acquaintances from industry association meetings or other events
- industry associations
- the media, predominantly the press.

It is important, therefore, when determining your target markets, to think laterally. Do not limit yourself to considering only direct clients, but examine in addition which types of companies might buy your services on behalf of their own clients, and which will also be influencers.

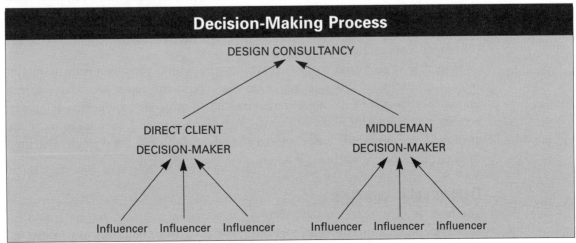

Depending on your design discipline, you might discover many middlemen, or none at all. You can then make a commercial decision on whether you want to include them in your target markets. Generally, for an established design company, it is preferable to work for direct clients: the chains of communication are shorter, and the fees will be higher. For newly launched design companies, however, middlemen can be not only a valuable source of income, but also a way of building your client list and your track record. Both direct clients and middlemen are best reached through bullseye, or direct, campaigns, which are described in Chapter 7.

There will always be an enormous number of influencers, and it is important to include them in your promotional programmes. However, because of the difficulties involved in identifying them precisely, they are best reached by broadshot, or indirect, campaigns, which are also outlined in Chapter 7.

A last small, but important, point on this subject. Design companies which form a part of a large communications or other group should remember to include key executives from sister companies as either middlemen or influencers, or both. Work does not flow automatically between companies in these situations: it is up to the individuals to earn it.

Geographical limits

Once you have settled on your target business sectors, however broad or narrow and however many or few, you will need to decide on the geographical limits for your marketing programme. To make an ambitious 'the world is my oyster' type of plan is admirable, but it is only any good if that plan can actually deliver the clients. Bear in mind that if you approach a potential client, you must be prepared to visit that client in their own offices for a sales meeting or credentials presentation, and to make several follow-up visits if things go well, all for no payment. Can you afford to risk the time and the money? Only do it if you can. It's not only potential overseas clients which can cause travelling difficulties. If there are only a few of you in your company, how much time can you afford to spend travelling to meetings? As a rule, the smaller your company, the smaller your geographical reach should be. The exception would be for a design consultancy which, by choice or accident, is located some distance away from any potential clients. By definition, this is likely to be well away from major city centres, and it could be argued that the expenditure on travelling is balanced by lower costs for office rent, rates and administration.

Does this mean that you only work for clients within your own realistic reach? No, of course not. What it means is that you only make pro-active, direct approaches to companies within that reach. If more distant potential clients contact you, having heard about you through word of mouth, then go to see them at once. They are already well disposed to you, and you stand a very good chance of obtaining work from them, if you can manage it profitably.

Demographic targeting

You have decided which business sectors you are going to tackle, and have defined the geographical limits of your programme, whether within one city or worldwide.

Now you need to define your target companies by demographics:
- a job title
- the company name
- area of commercial activity
- address, phone and fax details.

Demographic Identification		
Step 1	Which business sectors?	Private health care
Step 2	Which geographical limits?	Western Europe
Step 3	Which company names?	ABC, GHI, MNO
Step 4	Which titles and roles?	(i) managing director (ii) marketing director
Step 5	Which individual names?	ABC (i) Wilfred Wong
		(ii) Maria Eriksdottir
		GHI (i) Martin Schmidt
		(ii) Boris Sikorsky
		MNO (i) Sophie West
		(ii) Adam Lejeune

The title or role most likely to belong to the decision-makers you want to reach will depend on which design discipline you are offering. Industrial and interior design can have clients from many different departmental roles, depending on the scale of the project and the exact nature of the work required; increasingly, marketing directors are having a significant voice in the process. In graphics, a new corporate identity is usually instigated by a client company's middle management, approved by the most senior management, and implemented by fairly junior people. Annual reports and human resource literature each have fairly obvious clients, but there can still be surprises. In continental Europe, packaging design is usually dealt with by middle marketing management; in the UK, it is often relatively junior brand and product managers who have the responsibility.

If you are going to use broadshot (indirect) approach methods, this much information is all you will need. If, however, you intend to reach these people through a bullseye (direct) approach campaign, you will also need to know their names. As we have seen earlier, this named person can be a direct client or a middleman.

All of these pieces of information fall into the demographic category. Ways of obtaining such information are discussed in Chapter 10 when databases are examined.

The steps in demographic identification, which should be done in parallel for each target business sector you have chosen, are shown in the chart.

Psychographic targeting

If you want to be a little more sophisticated in the preparation of your target markets, you can use a technique called psychographic definition which is well established in advertising and consumer marketing, but which has only recently begun to be used in business-to-business fields. Demographics describe what we are, while psychographics describe how we feel about things: our attitudes, beliefs, opinions and behaviour.

It might be that your company's personality is more likely to attract a risk-taking, entrepreneurial client than one who would prefer the assurance of a set cultural framework, or vice versa. The interviews with the practitioners in Part II demonstrate that some of them have started to address this issue, and can define in psychographic terms the types of people they believe they will attract as clients.

The way to establish a psychographic profile for a target market is to take the demographic and add the word: '…who…'. It sounds deceptively simple, but it will absorb a lot of your thinking time.

One demographic description can give rise to a number of quite different psychographic profiles. See the chart for an example.

Psychographic Profiles

DEMOGRAPHIC		PSYCHOGRAPHIC
The managing director of one of Europe's leading retailers	WHO	is bored with the creative solutions offered by the average design consultancy, and who wants to be challenged
	or WHO	knows that the next two years are going to be make or break for his or her company (and own career) and needs the best possible retail design advice
	or WHO	feels cheated by high design fees and is looking for a basic, no-frills design company he or she can trust
	or WHO	realizes that his or her staff are wasting time, energy and funds briefing different designers to work on projects, and wants to form a long-term strategic relationship with a design company which can offer a full service

Demographic targeting will determine your choice of approach method, in particular which media you might use for advertising or PR, which directories you should consider being in, and which exhibitions and events you should attend. Psychographic targeting will lead you to select the most powerful sales propositions, which is the subject of our next chapter, and to use the right tone of voice in all of your spoken and written communications.

Activity 5

This activity will help you to think about which target markets are right for your company.

A Consider whether vertical or horizontal sectoring would be the most fertile strategy for your company. It will depend on (a) how many skills you can currently offer, or can easily supply through recruitment or association, and (b) how many different market sectors you already have, or would like to have, some experience in. It is always a good idea to list the markets you and your colleagues currently enjoy, and start from there: if you feel uncomfortable in or bored by or morally opposed to a certain business sector, you will never produce your best work for it.

B List the types of middlemen who might purchase design from you on behalf of clients in your defined business sectors. Even if you think that you do not want to accept work from a third party, it is worth identifying them at this point, since they will in any case influence your direct potential clients, and might well be in a position to make a positive recommendation or referral. It is important to know who they are.

C List all of the influencers who might affect the judgement of a decision-maker working in these business sectors.

D Think about your geographical limits, remembering that it is often quicker, cheaper and easier to travel from one capital city to another than it is to travel the length or breadth of the same country.

E Start to isolate your target market by company and by individual title or role. It will, of course, take a lot of desk research before you can complete your final plan, which will include their names. For the moment we are thinking strategically: just get used to the principles.

F Consider the psychographic profile of potential clients who are more likely to want to work with you than with your closest competitors. Refer back to your list of hot competitors in Activity 3.

On the practices of marketing design services abroad

MAXINE JAYNE HORN: THE BRITISH DESIGN INITIATIVE

- Most British design companies' international marketing efforts consist of picking up the phone to an overseas client and saying, very slowly: 'Hello. Do you speak English?'

If you want to sell design services overseas, the first thing to do is to analyse the geographical markets and work out what you want from them. Does your chosen market have a long lead time for buying UK design, like Asia, or a short lead time, like Scandinavia? Is it fertile or infertile for your type of design? For example, the States is generally an infertile market for UK packaging design companies, unless an American company wants to export to Europe. Does the market traditionally pay high or low fees? Is it likely to provide a long- or a short-term opportunity?

The next thing to understand is how clients in different markets buy design, and why they might want to buy from you. In some countries, for example India and South America, clients are less experienced and tend to need more hand-holding, which takes more of your time. When you work in an overseas market, you usually have to step not only into their business culture in terms of their ethics and management practices, but also into their social culture. This is where it can help to have an agent. Some overseas clients, however, want to be more UK-oriented, and it is important to know and to understand the difference. If you are not able to adapt, stick to the multinationals.

You cannot export successfully from the UK. You have to leave the country, and you have to go back to a market time and time again if you are going to achieve a deal. It's therefore critical that you do a risk analysis on every opportunity. How much will it cost? It can help to link sales trips to exhibitions and conferences. Can you afford to be out of the office for the travelling time as well as the meeting time? Having said that, it is quicker to get to Paris from London than it is to get to Scotland. Generally, it is best to concentrate on one country at a time, and to develop your business from that country to one next door to it. Think long term.

Finding an agent is one route; forming a link with a company with mutually compatible business skills is another. In each case, you will need to have clear contractual arrangements. There is always a honeymoon period with any business relationship; try to give it six to 12 months to set a proper business plan and objectives. It is particularly important to agree who is responsible for selling the partnership, otherwise you might end up with nothing but another address on your letterhead, in which case it would be cheaper to get a post office address in the country concerned and have the postman as your partner.

We are very lucky as Brits that English is recognized as an international business language. However, if you are selling to a national of another country, you need ideally to be able to do it in their own language. If you have a brochure in other languages, don't forget that you need to be able to respond to sales enquiries in those same languages. It is only when your offer is something that a potential foreign client wants enough to seek you out, that language becomes less of a problem.

You will need to get the best possible commercial and legal advice, and it will differ from country to country. For example, with architectural and major interior projects, some clients will stipulate that you work with local contractors, use local employment law and remuneration policies. You will also usually be responsible for an agent's tax bill. It is helpful to get advice before you start on which export and other grants, such as for research, are available from the government via the Department of Trade and Industry.

Finally, once a prospect becomes a client and the contracts are all agreed, it is the cost of servicing that client which becomes the main issue. The costs of sales visits to other companies in that same country get progressively lower as you combine trips and meetings.

As the home market becomes increasingly competitive, UK design companies should turn to exports. However, time, cost and commitment should not be under estimated: seek advice, do your homework and, above all, forget you're British.

The British Design Initiative (BDI) is a commercial organization which offers specialist export services to UK design companies, including overseas market research, appointment setting, design events, publicity and new business development. It also offers the Strategic Design Alliance, which identifies compatible business partners worldwide. For further information, contact The British Design Initiative, Burlington House, 184 New Kings Road, London SW6 4NF, UK.

6 WHY SHOULD THEY BOTHER?
DEVELOPING SALES PROPOSITIONS

'It is not only fine feathers that make fine birds.'
Aesop: *Fables* 'The Jay and the Peacock'

- Meaningful propositions
- Features and benefits

Meaningful propositions

If you have identified your positioning and your demographic target markets carefully, you have taken two steps towards creating a series of strong sales propositions. If you have also thought about the psychographic profile of that target market, add another step. If you understand a target individual well enough to work out what, if anything, will make them decide to appoint you as their design consultancy, you are nearly there.

Sales propositions are the statements you make to a potential client in order to convince him or her that your consultancy is the right choice for the work in question, or – if the timing means that there is no immediately available work from that source – that your consultancy should be borne in mind so that you will be the right choice when the next opportunity arises. They can either be made overtly to a potential client, or understood by implication. The balance is critical: if you trot out too many reasons for using your consultancy, you will be seen as a pushy salesman. If, on the other hand, you assume that the person you are talking to knows all about you, and fail to come up with any propositions at all, you won't get the work.

In consultancy, unlike in consumer goods or more basic business-to-business services (such as stationery or equipment supplies), the very best sales propositions do not shout. In a way, they are always heard and believed, but rarely actually noticed. Good sales propositions are quietly and skilfully slipped into a conversation or into a written document. They act as 'invisible salesmen' for your company and services. As was noted in Chapter 3, it is important to remember that none of us like to feel that we are being sold to. We prefer to convince ourselves that we have made the right decision through a process of rational analysis and commercial instinct.

The term USP, or Unique Selling Proposition, was coined by the American advertising industry in the 1940s, and it still plagues many marketing strategies. It is based on the existence of inimitable – or previously unclaimed – product features. In other words, what can you offer that no one else can match, or has previously stated that they offer? It is difficult for any design company to come up with a truly unique proposition. Fortunately, in order to work in the design market, sales propositions do not have to be unique. They do, however, have to be meaningful. They need to address both the rational needs and the emotional desires of the person you are trying to reach, and they must be as tightly focused as possible on the chosen target individual. For example, the things which attract a client at the beginning of their career are often different from those which appeal to them later on. Equally, the reasons for choosing one design supplier over another might be quite different in other circumstances or at other times. Perhaps, for design, the term should be not USP, but MSP: Meaningful Sales Proposition.

It is important to remember that all sales propositions also have to be deliverable. If you manage your clients' expectations badly, you should not be surprised if they are disappointed with the experience of working with you. Or to put it more simply, if you fail to fulfil your promises, you will not be asked again. This might seem like obvious advice, but it is very easy when putting together an entrepreneurial marketing plan to get carried away with visions of your own glory. See Chapter 12 for more information on this subject.

To start, you should aim to develop general sales propositions which become so familiar to you and to every member of your company that you don't even have to stop to think about them. Many of the practitioners interviewed for Part II of this book are so well versed in their company's selling language that it runs as a leitmotif through everything they say: see how many you can spot. General sales propositions should be developed in such a way that they attract your widest band of defined target clients.

On top of these general sales propositions, however, you will need to think about specific ones to put to a particular market sector, and then to a particular company or organization, and then to a particular title or role in that company. What, for example, are the benefits of working with you which are likely, as far as you can judge, to convince people to work with you? What might a 25-year-old male brand manager in a British wines and spirits company believe? Which arguments would a 39-year-old female human resources director of a major German airline listen to? What is a 43-year-old male managing director of a chain of French fashion shops going to need? What would sway a 57-year-old male chairman of an Italian electrical goods manufacturer?

For bullseye approaches, of course, you will also have to think about specific propositions to put to an individual. What might convince William Brown, Wilhelm Braun, Guillaume LeBrun or Guilliemo Bruno working in those roles? Further, what would convince Mary White, Geoff Green and Susan Black, all brand managers working in the same company as William Brown? The more sophisticated you get in your marketing, the greater the need for increasingly direct communications.

Features and benefits

All sales propositions, whether general or specific, must be based on benefits, and not on features. In the words of many a sales textbook: 'Features tell, benefits sell.'

Sometimes it is difficult for design companies to think beyond features, particularly if they fall into the product-focused category, as outlined in Chapter 1. Their sales letters, brochures and credentials presentations all start (and sometimes continue and end) with features. For example:

- we have been established for ten years
- we design consumer products/electronic engineering/supermarkets/office interiors/brochures/identities/packaging
- we have offices in London and Prague
- we employ 20 people
- we have invested in the latest technology
- our clients include Megacorp International, Eurobiz, Global Goodies and Intergalactic Sectors.

As features, the above statements are fine. There is nothing wrong with them at all; they just don't go far enough. They need to be turned into benefits.

Benefits – which form the basis of sales propositions – will always stem from features; in fact, you cannot have a benefit which is not firmly rooted in a feature. However, one feature can give rise to more than one benefit, and different people might perceive different benefits in the same feature. A car might have a sun roof; that is a feature. The benefit to one person might be that it provides draught-free ventilation. To another, it might be the supply of sunshine and fresh air. To a third, it might be the feeling it gives of driving an open-top car without any of the security and safety disadvantages. Or it could be all of these things to a fourth person.

To turn a feature into a benefit, there is a simple trick: you add the words: 'So that …' to the feature. Let's try it with all of the features we listed above:

FEATURE		BENEFIT
We have been established for ten years	so that…	you can be confident that we are an experienced, commercially viable company which knows what it is doing and which will not fold in the middle of a project
We design (whatever speciality)	so that…	you can benefit from our expertise in that area
We have offices in London and Prague	so that…	you can rely on us to view your projects with an international eye or your export programmes can benefit from our Eastern European experience
We employ 20 people	so that…	you can relax in the knowledge that we are large enough to have the necessary staff infrastructure for your project or you benefit from the compact nature of our company, which allows senior level input into all of our work
We have invested in the latest technology	so that…	you will save money or you will save time

Our clients include (whatever names)   so that...

or

the most up-to-date presentation of your product will be available to you you can be assured that we have worked for equally large/high profile companies as yours

or

you know that other companies you admire have chosen to work with us; can they all be wrong?

50

In the end, your sales propositions should fall into two parts: the general propositions which would attract anyone in your broadest target area, and series of parallel specific propositions for each of the subdivisions into more narrowly defined sectors. The more horizontal your approach, the more parallel propositions you will have. To take this further, you will have additional propositions to make to particular companies in those sectors, to titles or roles in those companies, and finally to individual names. See the chart for a graphic representation of this process.

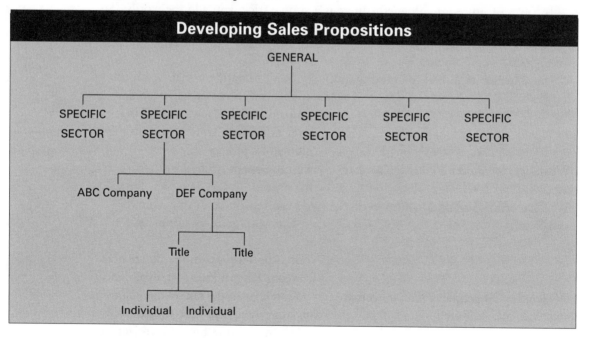

Activity 6

This activity will help you to develop sales propositions for your company. Remember that they must be both meaningful and deliverable, and that they should be based on benefits, not features.

A Develop general sales propositions for your company. What would persuade anyone in your broadest target market to consider appointing you?

B Now develop propositions which are:

- specific to a business sector
- specific to one company or organization in that sector
- specific to one title or role in that company or organization
- specific to one individual person.

Do this exercise with a recent potential client in mind: if you cannot, do it for an existing client.

C Repeat exercise B for each of your chosen client individuals, titles, companies and business sectors. Are the specific propositions you think of different in each case?

7 HOW WILL THEY FIND OUT ABOUT YOU? APPROACH METHODS

'Only connect!'
E M Forster: *Howards End*

- The two toolkits
- Broadshot methods
- Bullseye methods
- Word of mouth, referrals and recommendations
- Networking works

The two toolkits

You have two communication toolkits at your disposal, two basic means of delivering your sales message to your defined target market. Both of the toolkits and the tools they contain are essential parts of any good marketing programme. Neither of them, however, will actually obtain any business for you on their own: it is up to you to convert the people you have contacted through good presentations and through sales and negotiation skills. Any approach method can only help you to make that first connection.

The first toolkit contains broadshot approaches, where you put a focused proposition to a group of people with similar interests, but not to named individuals. This is sometimes referred to as indirect marketing. Its aim is to create, alter, improve and maintain your company's profile in your chosen marketplace, and it will help you to achieve a certain 'top-of-mind' quality among your target audience. It is a one-way means of communication: in other words, once you have decided to do it, it will take place whether anyone is looking and listening or not. It will give you delayed feedback, but only if you remember to include a response mechanism or to ask people contacting you how or where they got your details from. It is a bit like setting out a market stall with all of your best wares on it and then waiting for customers to inspect the merchandise. It is a passive, impersonal form of selling and yet it can be very powerful: if you get it right, potential clients will contact you.

Examples of tools in the design market's broadshot kit are:
- PR through the media
- advertising and inserts in publications
- mail which is not addressed to an individual
- directories
- passive IT and electronic media channels (Internet, World Wide Web etc)

- registers
- exhibitions and trade shows
- sponsorship
- personal appearances at events, as participant or attender
- awards.

The second toolkit contains bullseye approaches, where you put a focused proposition to a targeted, named individual. It involves a highly skilled, one-to-one approach. This is sometimes referred to as direct marketing, but the term bullseye is preferable, as 'direct marketing' often includes activities which are indirect, or broadshot, such as direct response advertising and mailed items addressed only to a title or a role and not to an individual person. A bullseye approach aims to make contact with another person. It is a two-way means of communication, and it will give you immediate feedback, whether positive or negative. It is an interactive form of selling: you make personal contact with potential clients. It is just as powerful as the broadshot approach.

The tools in the design market's bullseye kit are:
- PR through personal contact
- telephone contact
- mail.

Each of these broadshot and bullseye tools offers different strengths and weaknesses; they do different jobs. Each is valid, but not a straight replacement for another. They work best in combination, as we will see when we look at putting together an implementation plan in Chapter 8. Let's review them each in turn.

Broadshot methods

1 PR through the media

A design story will have to be very interesting, unusual or informative to appear in a national medium. However, despite this difficulty, there are an increasing number of good quality national radio and television programmes about designers and their work, which is encouraging.

These are the opportunities open to the design industry for reaching decision-makers and influencers through the media, ranked in order of likelihood of anything from or about your company ever appearing:
- the design trade press
- client sector trade press
- local press
- local radio and television
- national press
- national radio and television.

Journalists have a job to do: to provide news, features, information, opinions and stories to their readers or viewers. They are not a part of your PR team: often, what is interesting to them is what you don't want them to find out about. Having said that, journalists need you – or at least they need you to give them your stories, to suggest articles and features to them. They are as nervous of a blank computer screen as you are. If they know you, they will not do you any favours, but they will be more prepared to talk to you, and they will often phone you for comments on a subject for which they are writing an article.

The first thing to do, therefore, is to form a good relationship with the people working on the publications and programmes that your potential clients read or watch, as well as the ones which you read or watch. If you have local clients, contact your local media business pages or programmes. If not, forget all about local media opportunities. If you want to get your company's name and services into the minds of widget manufacturers, you should be concentrating your energies on the sector's own trade press – *Widget Weekly* or whatever. The design and creative press is important for increasing the motivation of your staff (it increases the feeling of belonging), for influencing the best potential recruits (who want to work for a company they've heard of, and think well of), and for reaching the small number of potential clients who are very design focused, and therefore read the design and creative magazines.

Always see your choice of media from a potential client's viewpoint, and then think about what that medium would be interested in. Remember that the media is not only about news. A weekly trade magazine, for instance, has interviews, articles, opinion pieces or private views written by readers, and quite possibly an active letters page, as well as a couple of pages of news. Do your research carefully, look for opportunities, and do not waste everyone's time by sending out inappropriate material.

How do you find out who to contact to start building that relationship? Newspapers and magazines print lists of their permanent staff, usually on the same page as the address and publishing details. Radio and television stations will tell you the names of the key people working on specific programmes if you phone them.

There are some universal guidelines to follow:

- It is surprising how small in number the editorial teams are, especially on monthly publications. Make a note of which person is responsible for which area of the publication: if you send news to the features editor, it might be handed over the desk to a colleague, but it is just as likely to be handed to the wastepaper bin.

- Try to make a journalist's life easier by providing information in the form they want it: ask them, and also use your common sense.

- Learn about deadlines. The hottest story is useless five minutes after a paper has gone to press, or after a programme has gone out on air. You will then have to wait for the next edition, and your story will appear as analysis if the content has not already gone cold.

- Learn not to bother a journalist on press day or during the hours before broadcast. Think how you feel about photocopier salesmen phoning you on the day of a major pitch.

- For press, send photographs of work or people whenever possible, in a form that the publication can use; ask them what they would like. It pays to invest in the best quality photography that you can afford, remembering that the shots can be used for many other purposes.

- Always give more than one contact name, and make sure that all of the people whose names are listed are fully briefed on the subject matter. Journalists do not simply print a press release; they need to have more information and quotes.

- Never, ever, hassle a journalist, break promises or lie. They are human beings and, like the rest of us, they have understandably long memories.

Media stories are a blend of news and views. Sometimes it can be helpful to generate news by, for example, conducting a research study on a subject which will be of interest to others and offering the results to the media.

What makes a good media story can often depend on the medium. The more general the publication or programme, the bigger the need for an impactful content or viewpoint. The more technical it is, the more interested it will be in details, in the 'how' of what you have done. They all have particular readerships or audiences: try to think about what would interest them.

One story might therefore have quite a range of applications. For example, the successful design of a new range of domestic furniture made from recycled banana skins might be interesting to a national television programme on future technology, a national radio programme on environmental issues, a national newspaper's 'small business/entrepreneurship' section, a local radio show about local business successes, an international trade furniture magazine and a national creative publication. However, although it is possible to have your story appear in several different places, you need to recognize that exclusivity within their own sector is important to editors as an indication of the quality of their product.

Obviously, no medium can ever give you a guarantee that your contribution will actually be used: journalists themselves have to quickly get used to the pain of seeing their work discarded at the last minute. According to Ken Gofton, the Special Projects Editor of UK's *Marketing*, writing on the subject of media relationships:

> If your story isn't used, or appears in a form you don't recognise, there could be several reasons:
> (a) it has been squeezed out by something more interesting
> (b) you got the timing wrong and missed the deadlines
> (c) you failed to explain the significance of your mega-breakthrough to the dim-witted hack
> (d) your press announcement was boring, incomprehensible, incredible or misdirected
> (e) other sources – independent or competitive – suggested you were talking a load of old cobblers
> (f) plain editorial incompetence.
> Persevere.

He ends his article with a comment that, for me, sums up why it is worth making an effort with media relations:

> The field of press relations is complex, frustrating, and carries no guarantee of success. On the other hand, there seems little doubt that the companies which take it seriously, and take steps to raise their profile, reap the benefit – particularly in a climate of extreme competition.

2 Advertising and inserts in publications

For design companies, advertising means taking space in business-to-business publications, or sections of publications. Other media such as television, radio and posters are too widely focused to be cost-effective.

Press advertising and inserts belong together because, in terms of the choice of a publication for either, the parameters are the same. Inserts have a disadvantage compared with advertisements in that they tend to fall out of a magazine. Many readers simply throw them out without even glancing at them. On the other hand, they have certain advantages. They can be a little more impactful visually, perhaps incorporating elements of paper engineering. They can also be kept by readers for future use, filed away like a mini-brochure. If you are thinking of inserts, make sure that they are so special that people will not want to bin them immediately.

If you are going to invest in either, you will find that the entry costs are high; it therefore pays to know what you are doing. Again the choice of publication is critical. Which papers or magazines do your potential clients read? After you've established that, the process of selection is fairly straightforward.

All publications have rate cards which will tell you how much they charge for space: it will vary according to the size of your advertisement, where it is situated in the magazine, and whether you want colour, mono or spot colour. If you are going to book a series, it is possible to negotiate a volume discount. The publication's advertising sales department will also be able to provide you with information on the publication's circulation, which will be expressed demographically, usually by job title. Actual readership can be significantly lower or higher than circulation. A magazine can have free circulation, paid circulation (in which case people are more likely to read it, as they have actively chosen it), or a combination of both. When assessing costs, the important thing is not the actual cost of the space, but something called the comparative Cost Per Thousand (CPT), that is the cost of reaching one thousand people in your desired target audience group. For example, a low-cost space which reaches 50 members of your target market will prove to be considerably more expensive than a higher-cost space which reaches several thousand.

The publication will also send you details of the production department's requirement for artwork. They are almost always very helpful with their advice and, if you are a non-graphic design company, you might find it useful to know that some will be able to produce advertisements for you at an extra price. You will, however, have to supply the ideas and copy.

There is a commonly held but mistaken view that advertising does not work for design consultancies. However, it will only work if you manage it properly. To be successful, advertising or inserts must be:

i *Part of a long-term strategic campaign*
   There is little point in running one advertisement and then sitting back and waiting for the phone to ring. It won't, unless you are trying to get business with a sales promotion, such as half-price design, or free trips to Hawaii for every client. Business-to-business advertising will slowly build the awareness that you exist and impart a limited amount of information about what you are offering.

It will lay the foundations for the rest of your marketing, so that when you first contact a prospect, they will have heard of you beforehand.

ii *Regular*

There are two types of campaign: burst and drip. They are exactly as they sound, and may be used in combination. A burst campaign, concentrated and high-impact, works well for the launch of a new product or service. A drip campaign, with smaller spaces at regular intervals, will tend to be the more effective in the design market, as it will give your target audience a greater number of chances to see and register your message. A drip campaign will give a greater frequency or more Opportunities To See (OTS), as the advertising industry calls it, over a longer period of time.

iii *Consistent*

If you change your visual and verbal message with every appearance, you will be a contender for the annual Puzzle-a-Prospect Award. Have different advertisements or inserts by all means, but make sure that you keep them in the same communication family. A small number of design companies has successfully created excellent long-term advertising campaigns in this way in the marketing press. Very many more have simply wasted their money.

iv *Generous with contact information*

Have a clear response mechanism. You might want a tear-off or cut-out coupon, coded so that you know which publication it has come from. You could try freepost or freephone to increase the likelihood of responses. However, at a very minimum, you must have at least one contact name, an address, fax and telephone numbers, and your Internet address if you are on-line.

3 Mail which is not addressed to an individual

This approach performs the same function as an insert, but without the borrowed credibility of the publication. It is a waste of time and money and, worse, an insult to prospective clients. You are trying to sell a quality service; you should be providing quality communications. How much time would it take to phone and find out the name of the person currently holding the title you are writing to? Not very long. How long would it take for the non-personalized mailshot to hit the bin? Slightly less.

4 Directories

There are two kinds of directories: those which are separate publications, whether printed or digital, and those which are found at the back of magazines.

If you take space in a directory, apply exactly the same selection criteria as for media advertising. To whom is it distributed? What is the cost per thousand? Never agree to taking space without first seeing a copy of the directory. Even if the space is free – as with a lot of directory space – think carefully. The main question to ask yourself is whether or not a particular directory environment is right for your image. The good directories to be in are the ones issued by design trade bodies as they carry additional authority; the inclusion of your company is one of the advantages of membership.

On a separate, but important, point, remember that your presence in a directory under a design heading immediately notifies criminals that you are likely to have expensive computer equipment in your studio.

5 Passive IT and electronic media channels (Internet, World Wide Web etc)

How can such a dynamic and new medium as the Internet be passive? Because it relies on viewers wanting to find you, or coming across you by accident while they are looking for something else. A Web site – the multimedia part of the Internet, with graphics and sound – performs much the same function as a display advertisement, insert or directory. Through it, you will be able to tell people that you exist, what you do and how to find you. You need, therefore, to consider the same issues. Who does it reach? Is it the right image environment?

One advantage of a Web site is that you can constantly update the content. Another is that you can involve the reader through a more creative use of information provision. However, a significant disadvantage is the lack of feedback, and the resultant poor potential for database building. Although your service provider might be able to tell you how many people have visited your site, you will never know who they are, unless they have entered their own contact details in response to a request from you.

Incidentally, the more interesting you make it graphically, the greater the problem of speed of access to your site. Are you really going to ask potential clients to wait anything up to half an hour to download your file? It pays to subcontract the design and installation of your site to a specialist designer, and to look carefully at what the different service providers are offering in terms of advice and maintenance.

In conclusion, it is worth considering passive electronic media as an adjunct to your main campaign, but it is too early yet to rely on it as a major method of communication. The trouble is that the medium is developing so rapidly that whatever one advises is soon out of date.

6 Registers

Clients sometimes like to source a design consultancy through a register, for which service they usually pay a fee. Registers provide clients with a greater degree of confidentiality than if they had to approach a number of designers, and protect them from the hounding they believe they will get if a design company knows that they are interested. In practice, many design companies never even follow up an enquiry, so it is perhaps an ill-founded worry.

Government or local council-managed registers come and go according to the availability of funding and differ widely in quality from country to country but they are worth looking into. Commercial registers also exist in several countries within search-and-select consultancies, and provide a good service for both the design companies on their databases and the clients who are looking. Some registers act rather like brokers, matching resources to needs; others more like associations which actively promote their members.

If you are considering registering with an organization, find out as much as you can about how they work, and what you will get for your fee. Ask also for examples of the results they have achieved for their members and, if you can, talk to companies already on the register to hear their opinion. One way to do this is through the people you meet at industry associations; one of the many good things about the design world is our willingness to share information with each other.

7 Exhibitions and trade shows

These are excellent ways to display your skills and to engage potential clients in conversation, to begin a dialogue which will last long after the duration of the show. They provide a controlled method of reaching a highly targeted marketplace. For some disciplines, such as industrial design, they form a regular part of the annual promotional programme.

It might sound obvious, but the first thing to sort out is how many potential clients are likely to visit an exhibition in which you are thinking of taking a stand. The organizers will supply you with rate card data very similar to those from the printed or broadcast media. For example, if your target market is marketing directors, look carefully at the indicated numbers for the past attendance of people with that title: what are they marketing directors of? Clients, competitors or suppliers? Exhibitions and trade shows will attract all three. Again, as with media and directories, the entry cost is high. Work out the cost per thousand, and try to visit a show before you decide to take part in it.

Exhibition stands are not cheap to produce, so take professional advice if you are not a specialist in that discipline; the organizers are also a good source of advice and help. Your stand must be of a sufficient quality to reflect well on your company, as must the people you put on it: they should be your very best sales people.

Don't have a lot of expensive brochures on display – they will disappear into free carrier bags never to be seen again, and you will have failed to capture any data on who has them. Ask visitors to the stand for business cards instead so that you can post brochures out later and, at the same time, grow your database.

Finally, look after the security of your stand and equipment. It's surprising how many things can disappear either during a show or at the end. The chairman of a packaging design company once said to me: 'When we were packing up, I took some of our products out to the car, and when I returned, our potted plants had gone. I went around the back of the stand to see if I could see where they were, and returned to discover that our very expensive glass fridge had disappeared.' Guard, and insure.

8 Sponsorship

Does this mean sponsoring the next World Cup? Of course not. Does it mean looking for creative and cost-effective ways to get your company's name in front of your target market in an appropriate and memorable way? Yes, it does. Don't think only of the design environment: what about sponsoring a prize or a competition or an award for clients? Or linking your name with a regular media column on your subject. For example, at the time of writing, UK's *Marketing* magazine has a 'Campaign of the Week' column sponsored by advertising agencies and a 'Design Choice' column sponsored by design companies. Why not invent your own, and approach a publication?

9 Personal appearances at events, as participant or attender

This is often seen as a form of PR, but in fact it is one of the most sophisticated forms of one-to-one marketing. It works: we all feel more comfortable doing business with people we have met.

We also like to do business with people who have achieved a certain status in their chosen field. Speaking at conferences is one way to add stature to your offer, but not all conference speakers are chosen because they are already famous. Some are asked because of their association with a trade or industry body, others put themselves forward to event organization companies. Naturally, this last route is very much easier if you are able to employ a PR person to do it for you.

Just going to events which potential clients are likely to attend can be surprisingly productive, but only if you make the effort to talk to people, and do not try to sell to them. There are not many things as unattractive at an event as someone who keeps trying to thrust their business card or brochure between your vol-au-vent and your glass of wine. If you meet someone who you would like to meet again in a more commercial context, remember who they are and write to them or phone them. It never takes too much research work: basic information is easily available.

10 Awards

There are people who never win competitions or raffles; often it is because they never enter any. The same is true of awards. Some companies win a lot of awards, both for creativity and effectiveness. What is the secret of their success? There are two things which they all do: firstly, their work is of the highest quality, and they fully deserve to win. Secondly, and importantly, they treat awards as a marketing priority, and take the time, trouble and expense involved in preparing entries as a part of their working operation, while others cannot be bothered. As an added benefit, the process of entering an award competition can strengthen your relationship with your client; designers are not the only people to enjoy winning.

Bullseye methods

1 PR through personal contact

PR in its widest meaning is public relations, not press relations. Who is your public? Your target market or markets? Although entertainment, or corporate hospitality, is used successfully by several business sectors, very few design companies promote themselves by taking potential clients to up-market sporting events and other glamorous events, or even by taking people out to long and expensive lunches. Why? Because most design company clients are far too busy and serious-minded – just like the design companies themselves – to be enticed by such gilded promises, and many people are uncomfortable with the idea of what they see as personal bribes and incentives. The best way to entertain clients and prospects if you want to get them together on a social basis, is to throw a party to celebrate a milestone in your company's development: for example, the launch of a new structure, or a new identity, or a significant anniversary.

There are other opportunities for providing both your clients and your potential clients with a reason to meet you on an occasion which is removed from a straightforward sales meeting. Clients enjoy meeting other clients, especially those working in the same or similar fields, and also enjoy broadening their field of knowledge. Several design companies, for instance, hold training courses for junior clients on design management. Others put together seminars or workshops on commercial subjects which would be attractive to more senior people. You could hold discussion breakfasts, lunches or dinners on a given business topic, perhaps chaired by a leading journalist in the clients' sector. Or you could hold evening debates, with key speakers from outside your company. The key thing is to issue an invitation which has added value. The invitation, by the way, is as important as the acceptance. Not everyone will be able to attend, but they will appreciate being asked.

2 Telephone contact

Together with mail, the use of the telephone is prevalent in business-to-business marketing. It performs two communications functions: inbound and outbound.

Inbound telephone marketing refers to the process by which enquiries are handled. Exactly how you do it will depend on the culture and personality of your own company, but here are a few general guidelines.

i   Think about the first point of contact for incoming calls, and how that person should handle those calls. Whoever picks up the phone, at whatever time of day, must know what to do. This therefore includes all temporary staff, especially those on switchboard and/or reception, and every member of permanent staff who is likely to answer the phone when the switchboard is not in operation. Not surprisingly, many potential clients will call at a time which suits them, often outside regular working hours. If you are marketing yourself to target markets in countries other than your own, consider the implications of time zone differences. Think also about what happens when everyone has gone home. What does your answerphone message say? More importantly, have you got an answerphone and is it always switched on at night? As part of a recent training project, 12 design companies were telephoned one evening after hours, to see how they managed their systems. Only three had answerphones switched on, although subsequent research showed that all but two companies possessed one.

ii For every inbound request for information about your company, the details of the person enquiring should be captured. It is not enough to make a note of someone's name and address and send them a brochure. Wherever possible, calls should be put through to the person in charge of the marketing programme, who can use questioning skills to elicit as much information as possible, in order to provide the most appropriate response. That person should also find out how the enquirer got to know about your design company: if you don't know what is working for you, how can you assess the effectiveness of your activities? If the right person is not available, the caller's name and telephone number should be taken, and a promise given that someone will call them as soon as possible. If they resist, and ask to be sent a brochure – as do many callers who are only making general enquiries and do not want to be hassled by phone – the best response is to take their address and telephone details and promise to send them something. Then pass the details on to the main marketing person, who should phone them before sending out the most appropriate material. Never waste an opportunity to make direct contact with a person enquiring about your company.

iii Capture permanently the details of all enquiries on your database (see Chapter 10). A design company once posted brochures to potential clients following an advertising campaign by getting its receptionist to write the address details directly on to the envelope in order to save time. The envelope was then posted without transferring the information on to anything else.

iv Treat every enquiry with charm. Yes, it might be a competitive design company in disguise. How can you tell? They will sometimes be reluctant to give a phone number. Give them the information anyway. Never run the risk of being seen as unhelpful to a genuine potential client. What about students doing research for a project? Be helpful: they might grow up to be clients one day. If your publicity material is very expensive, and you do not want to send it to students, explain this, and say that they would be very welcome to make an appointment to come to your premises and sit in your reception area to view a sample copy. Very few will take you up on the offer, but at least you will have been helpful.

Outbound telephone marketing is the second type, and the one which seems to cause the most difficulties for design companies. It refers to the process by which you contact a named individual in order to encourage them to agree to a face-to-face sales meeting. It is not the same as telesales, which is the process by which goods or services are sold over the telephone: an example would be insurance renewals. Design is never sold to new clients as the result of telephone conversations alone.

Outbound telemarketing is what many people dread. We are reluctant to do it. We recognize that communication by telephone is very intrusive: people answer the phone at times when they would not take a personal interruption or spend time reading a letter. Moreover, we are afraid of the consequences of the call: we fear rejection, and we give up easily. 'I've tried,' we say, 'but I couldn't get through.' The whole activity of telemarketing consumes both time and skills. In order to make telephone contact with one unemployed person at home during the day, telemarketing professionals reckon that it takes five phone calls. How many calls before you make contact with someone who is already on the phone, in meetings, in other people's offices, in the car, on trains and planes, on the street, in shops, at lunch, ill, on holiday. Oh, and who also doesn't know who you are or why you want to take up the little spare time they have. As we all know, it is hard to make contact with people who do want to talk to you.

However, it is possible to succeed in telemarketing. You will need:

i   Time: enough to devote to the process regularly.
ii Persistence: like the US Mail, good telephone operators always get through, even if it takes a long time.
iii A good database: if your outbound data is poor, you will waste time. If your inbound data is poor, you will waste opportunities. See Chapter 10.
iv Sales skills: this does not mean pushy. No one will respond well if you hassle them.
v   A good telephone manner: a clear, attractive voice helps.
vi Patience: telemarketing is not for those who thrive on quick results.

What if you don't have all of these attributes? If you feel that you cannot learn or acquire them yourself through good telephone sales skills training courses, then it is best to employ someone else to do the job. Chapter 10 contains some arguments for and against employing internal and external people to help with the marketing task.

Even if you have got the necessary skills, you will still need to get past the gatekeepers. These are the obstacles, usually human, between you and the person you are trying to reach. Main switchboard operators are not a problem; they are paid to put calls through, not to fend them off. Personal secretaries, on the other hand, are briefed and trained to protect their bosses from unnecessary tasks. They are often your first, and sometimes your only, contact with the person you want to speak to; it is important to make friends with them and view them as joint target markets. If you cannot convince them, you will not be able to convince their bosses.

Increasingly, however, with direct lines and the reduction in the numbers of secretaries, you stand a good chance of getting through to the person first time, and so you should be prepared for that. The downside of this system is that you might just as easily get through to the person's answerphone or voicemail. If you do, turn the situation to your advantage and leave a message to say who you are and that you will call back. Use the occasion to start to build a relationship with the other person, but don't ask them to phone you without stating exactly why you have been trying to get in touch. I have had several messages in the last few years asking me to phone urgently someone I don't know, without a company name and with a telephone number I don't recognize. Of course I phone, from wherever I am in the country or the world; it could be significant. It always turns out to be a photocopier/stationery supplier/car dealer, and they do not get my business. In the great client-supplier chain of being – and don't forget that you have suppliers, and that your clients have clients – it is the supplier who is supposed to do the running.

3 Mail

Just like telemarketing, direct mail will not bring you business on its own: strategic design consultancy is not a mail-order operation. The objectives of sending something through the mail are:

- to establish awareness of your company
- to impart some information about your services
- to outline the benefits to that particular person of working with you
- to facilitate an agreement to a meeting

Within that overall objective, you will need to decide whether you want to run a wide or narrow focus campaign. With a wide focus programme, your aim is to reach as many people as possible. It is quantitative in nature, and you should not attempt to follow up with phone calls. Instead, think of it more as a very direct advertising campaign.

With a narrow focus programme, which is qualitative in nature, your aim is to reach a smaller number of people. Here, you should follow each mailing up with a phone call: see Chapter 8 on suggestions for a flow of mail and telephone approaches.

What can you send through the post to attract and retain people's attention? More than just a letter, that's certain. The decision will rest on whether you plan a wide or narrow focus campaign. You can send:

- mailers
- brochures
- updates
- newsletters
- samples of work
- copies of press articles.

- news of awards entered or won
- books written by you or otherwise
- summaries of relevant research reports
- information sheets on useful subjects
- seasonal cards and small gifts.

A one-off item can have an effect, but the real results are gained through a good mailing campaign which is regular. It should be viewed as a long-term programme, a drip technique (see the earlier section on advertising), and can be successfully used in conjunction with telephone marketing.

Finally, a note of caution. I believe that it is still unacceptable to try to contact a potential client by fax or by intrusive IT channels such as E-mail. My objections are partly to do with protocol, or with what are currently considered to be acceptable forms of communication between people who have never met. However, they are also to do with quality: the visual tone of your communication will say as much about you as the content. Even a plain paper fax lacks the visual and tactile charm of a crisp letter, and E-mail communications are simply second-generation telexes: fine for information but poor for persuasion.

For further information on the content of letters, see Chapter 9.

Word of mouth, referrals and recommendations

Within the whole area of approach methods, one important – but often neglected – source of business is that of recommendations and referrals. As we have already seen, word of mouth can be very powerful. It comprises the inbound part of your business development programme: it brings enquiries to your door. Some companies, particularly those which are very well-known or which do not have many competitors for their specialisms, or both, are very successful without apparently ever using outbound techniques. However, inbound enquiries do not simply occur of their own accord. Repeat business comes as a result of doing the best possible work for your clients, and providing excellent value for money and levels of service. Recommendations and referrals come from actual clients talking to other potential clients, and from other people talking about the fact that you do excellent work. The ideal situation is when a client, who was after all once a prospect, becomes a missionary for your company.

Referrals and recommendations, therefore, come from two main contact points:
i current and past clients
ii other professionals who have formed a view about your company through word of mouth.

The opinions that people hold of you can come from a variety of sources, the chief one being, of course, experience of working with you, either as a direct client or a third party who has commissioned you on behalf of their own clients (see Chapter 5). However, it is also possible that a potential recommender of your product and services might simply have heard about your offer and abilities through word of mouth, or that they have met you or other members of your company at an industry function. This is where a formal programme of networking can pay.

Networking works

Because we are human beings, we prefer to work with people we know, and of whom we have heard good things. An important part of your marketing efforts should include getting to know people, not only clients but also third parties and, of course, influencers. You need to meet people at industry events, at talks, at conferences. You need to join organizations and become an active member; you might even consider becoming part of a committee or task group at one of those organizations. In business, it remains true that it is both 'what you know' and 'who you know' which counts, and a good networking programme can help you to stay top-of-mind should a suitable opportunity arise.

As we have already seen earlier in this chapter, networking does not mean that you have to try to meet everyone in the room, thrusting business cards at them. It does mean, however, that you have to get out and about. As well as going to design events, go to as many of your clients' sectors events as possible, local, national and international.

Activity 7

This activity will teach you to be analytical about other peoples' broadshot and bullseye approaches. Try to get into the habit of looking critically, and learning.

A Hold a discussion session with a few other members of your company. Think about some of the goods and services which have been bought for your company (or alternatively which you have bought for yourselves) in the last 12 months.

- How did you learn about their existence in the first place? Was it through word of mouth, or through broadshot or bullseye approaches?
- Which decisions were the easiest to make? Did it depend on how you heard about them?

B Select one of your target client sectors, and get hold of all of the papers and magazines which might influence a potential client in that sector.

Analyse the stories which have appeared. How were they presented? What differences are there between publications? Try to work out which articles and features have appeared as a result of investigative journalism, and which as a result of information given to the media.

C With the same publications, analyse the advertisements which appear. Are they impactful? Informative? Persuasive? Would you be clear about how to get more information if you wanted it?

D Many people who are given the task of telemarketing have not had much experience as a recipient of sales calls. Those who have had the experience often get rid of the call as soon as possible without learning anything from them. From today, ask for all sales calls coming into the company to be put through to you. Listen and learn. You can always direct them to the right person afterwards. Which techniques seem to work best? Which techniques failed to convince you?

E Make a list of the kinds of events you could attend or organizations you could join in order to meet direct and third party clients and influencers.

On media relations

LYNDA RELPH-KNIGHT: EDITOR, *DESIGN WEEK*

- Make yourself accessible to phone calls from the press, nominate someone whose responsibility it should be. If you want publicity, you'll only get it by talking to people.

Someone phoned recently to complain that they had 'placed' some editorial with us, and it had not appeared. I had to gently point out to them that you do not 'place' editorial; you place advertising. You pay for advertising; you have complete control of it within the limits of the law and the advertising standards people. Editorial, on the other hand, is free. It is independent, it does no favours, and an editorial team will interpret information given to it in an appropriate way. You can't expect everything to be published verbatim: journalists will check the information out, and generally balance it with another view, another case.

The way to develop the best relationship with the press is through partnership. Try to understand our needs, for example our deadlines and the kind of news and special features we may be looking at. Get to know us. We are not here to do your PR, but it's only human nature that we go to the people we know for a comment on a specialist area, or for a piece on a particular issue. There's an element of trust. However, we wouldn't ever pull our punches if one of our regular contacts was doing something untoward, for example free-pitching.

Get to know the individual members of staff on any editorial team, and find out what their responsibilities are so that you always speak to the right person about the right subject. For example, don't bother the news editor on a busy press day about a feature idea when he or she isn't responsible for features anyway. They will probably remember that it was you who pestered them on the wrong day. Be active in the design community, because that way we will seek you out. Ring us and suggest that we meet if you've got something worth talking about. Pick up the phone, but choose the moment, choose the day.

Be proactive; come up with ideas. Don't wait for us to come to you and say: 'Ah, we've heard you're the world authority on stamp design.' Come to us and say that you have an interesting point of view on something, and ask to write an article or a comment on it. People who do that get some sort of showing in most journals, because they are prepared to say something that their peers will be interested in.

You can approach a magazine with something that you think is either hot news or a longer-term issue, but don't tout it about. It is very important to a publication to have material either first or exclusively; we all have our pride. Try it out on the publication you think is best for it. If they say 'No', then take it somewhere else, but give them a bit of time to decide. There's nothing more irritating for an editor thinking about running something than to see it appear in a rival title in a slightly different form. If you had done some packaging for a gardening product, say, I wouldn't necessarily know that you had sent the same story to a gardening magazine, but I would if you had sold it to a design or marketing title. Be broad in your coverage, but specific with your choice of magazine within a particular sector. It's helpful to remember that weekly publications are very news led, and they want that news ahead of the competition. Monthly journals are more interested in feature ideas.

How you send material to the press depends on what it is. If it's something big or important, it is worth a phone call first to the right person; you may then be asked to jot down a few notes. We generally prefer to have very brief information – unless it is a research report or similar – because we want to ask you our own questions. I wouldn't expect any reputable magazine to base all of its information on stuff that arrives in the office. We'd also want to know the name of the person we should contact, a list of credits of people that, in an ideal world, we ought to mention in connection with the work, and also contact details for a client if it is a question of project work.

There is a lot of wasted time and effort. We might receive a phone call saying that someone is about to fax a press release, and asking who to send it to. The fax comes, followed by a phone call to see if we got it, and then a hard copy in the post. We haven't yet had releases also appearing on the Internet, but I think that could be the next step. Then it's pester, pester, pester with phone calls – by which time the release has been in the bin a long time because the information wasn't interesting or relevant in the first place. Pestering is one of the things we react against, in the same way that clients react against having brochures sent to them persistently.

Generally, I would advise people against signing up PR agencies unless they know exactly what they want to get out of them. Our experience of agencies, particularly the bigger ones, is that they deal mainly with press releases and tick things off lists. They bombard us with information which may not be relevant, because they haven't researched the market. They sometimes have people working on accounts who don't know their clients; quite often, we tell them what their clients are doing. They can never be truly abreast of what you are up to because they've got ten similar clients on their books and they are not part of your culture. Partly it's to do with the way you brief them, partly it's the extent to which you include them in your team. Design is so people based, so much about personalities and culture. It is important to have someone promoting you who really knows where you're coming from.

That said, there is a handful of very good PR people in the design field and they have steered us towards some good and lasting relationships. The better ones tend to have worked in-house at a big design company. Some work independently for two or three clients who don't overlap, devoting one or two days a week to each. They have a desk in the office, and are part of the team and the culture.

If you do appoint an agency, you should still have someone in your company – preferably more than one person – who will respond to the press. As an editor, I would expect to deal with the senior people in consultancies, whether or not they have a PR agency. Keep responsibility for your own publicity, even though you may have an agency to do some of the work for you.

Overall, the best way for a design company to work with the media depends on the personality of the individual company. You should be aware that you have a personality, and approach us with that in mind. Don't send us great reams of worthy, printed material if you are a fun outfit. If you're fun, let us know, but get the information to us as well.

Design Week is the UK's only weekly publication to deal exclusively with design industry news and issues. It is part of the Centaur group, which also publishes *Marketing Week* and *Creative Review*. For further information contact *Design Week*, St Giles House, 50 Poland Street, London, W1V 4AX, UK.

8 I THINK, THEREFORE I PLAN: PUTTING IT ALL TOGETHER

'It is wise to look ahead, but difficult to look farther than you can see.'
Winston Churchill: *Observer* 'Sayings of the Week' 27 July 1952

- Integrated marketing
- Bullseye approaches
- Flow of bullseye approaches
- Implementation plans

Integrated marketing

Now that you have identified the four cornerstones of a workable marketing strategy – what you are, who wants you, why they should bother, and how they will find out about you – you can start to develop your implementation, or action, plan.

As in many business areas, a mixture of marketing approaches is more effective than a single route: the idea is to make the whole seem much larger than the sum of the parts. Prospective clients should feel that they have heard about you from a wide variety of sources, that your name keeps popping up everywhere they look. It is all about keeping your company's name (and preferably its positioning and proposition as well) top-of-mind. Many opportunities are lost simply because your name did not emerge from the prospective client's memory bank at the appropriate moment.

You will know yourself how frustrating it is to suddenly remember the name of the ideal supplier half way through a project, or to receive a reminder letter or telephone call from someone who would have been ideal for the job shortly after commissioning a less preferable person to do the work. If you can achieve a regular and consistent top-of-mindedness among your target individuals, at least you stand the chance of being considered once an opportunity does occur. This is why a drip (as opposed to burst) and integrated (as opposed to single-route) programme works so well for the marketing of design consultancy services.

It is just as important that existing clients, and dormant clients who have given you work in the recent past, but who you are not talking to on a daily basis, keep your company name top-of-mind so that they contact you as soon as an appropriate project presents itself. Chapter 12, which discusses client retention and development, will provide further information on marketing yourself to current and recent clients.

A mixture of approaches will allow you to tap into prospective and existing clients' streams of consciousness in a variety of ways. However, a wild assortment of ill-judged and ill-managed attempts will not work. In order to be effective, all of your approaches and your communications must be integrated. In practice, this means that they must:

- be timed to take place at regularly spaced intervals
- follow the same strategy
- include the same benefits to the same target sector
- be complementary in their messages
- be consistent in their visual and verbal tone of voice.

In integrated marketing, not only do you have to consider which combination of broadshot and bullseye approaches would be the most appropriate, but you should also try to allocate a weighting to each, a measure of importance, so that you can plan the relative time and budget resources you intend to put behind each type of approach. This should be done for each of your target sectors. You might discover, for example, that a broadshot campaign of profile-raising through a few specific press publications, plus a highly targeted programme of sales letters and telephone calls might be the best way to reach individuals in one target sector, while those in a different sector might be best reached through a broadshot annual exhibition plus bullseye personal contact PR. Only one thing is certain: there is no set way of developing a universal integrated marketing plan which will apply to every target sector. What is right for one could be a disaster if deployed against another.

Bullseye approaches

Within the two main bullseye approaches of mail and telephone (the third, PR through contact, will always involve one or the other), the thorny question of which you do first will inevitably crop up: do you phone then write, or write then phone?

There is a pattern of approaches which has been proven to work better than others. Although some marketing consultants would disagree – and they are usually those who are heavily committed to cold telephone prospecting – it is best to write a letter first to the person concerned, and then follow it up with a phone call, followed by a letter, and so on. You will then start to see a pattern of contacts emerging, a flow, which leads to a dialogue. It is a very direct, very personal system, and it can be sustained over a long period of time when necessary.

After the first postal and telephone conversations have taken place, which form the Active Approach (AA) phase, you will move into a longer term, Keep In Touch (KIT) phase. Here, you should aim to send regular mailings of different sorts, preferably every three months. For certain potential clients, you might want to add the occasional KIT phone call but, on the whole, a regular mailing programme is more effective. Not only is it less expensive for you in terms of time spent than long-term telephone campaigns, but it avoids the danger of being perceived as a nuisance, or telephone pest.

Naturally, all of your AA and KIT contacts will also be affected by any broadshot marketing activities you undertake, such as PR through the media, or directory entries, or advertising programmes, or speaking at conferences.

Flow of bullseye approaches

How does this pattern, this flow, actually work in practice? See the chart overleaf for a good, workable AA and KIT plan.

You can see from the chart that AA and KIT approaches pursue a logical system of relationship marketing. From bringing a contact to the boil through a very direct and immediate AA phase, you then keep the relationship on simmer through your extended KIT programme for as long as necessary.

The result from your first letter, which should be sent without any other material such as a mailer, a brochure or samples (you will want to save those for another occasion), will be one of three possible outcomes. The prospect will either say 'Yes – come and see me', usually by phoning you; 'No – I am not interested at all/at present', which is usually a written reply, particularly from those companies and organizations which have a quality or standards requirement to answer every letter they receive; or, most commonly, there will be no reply.

If the answer is 'Yes' – and indeed whenever you achieve a 'Yes' response throughout the duration of the approach programme – you should proceed to the presenting and pitching stage as outlined in Chapter 11. The result will inevitably be that you either get work, or you do not.

If the answer to your first letter is 'No' in writing, phone the person concerned to express your disappointment, and ask whether you can send them some information about your company, in case the need should arise in the future. If the answer is 'No' by an inbound telephone call, which is rare, use that phone call to have the same conversation. At this point, your objective is simply to make contact, to start to build a personal relationship and, ultimately, to make sure that the person is placed on your KIT programme for future opportunities; you are unlikely to convert the phone call into an agreement to a meeting. If you do not get a reply at all to your first letter, phone the person concerned. As always, you will get one of the same three responses identified above: 'Yes', 'No' or no contact (the telephone equivalent of no reply).

If you do not manage to make direct telephone contact after three attempts, during which you might have talked to the person's assistant, or have left a message on a voicemail, stop phoning. There comes a point when a different tactic is required. Write your second letter, which can now contain a mailer, or a brochure, or samples of work. Again, you will get one of the three by now familiar responses.

If you receive a 'No' or do not get a response, make a second batch of three phone calls at most: depending on the outcome, either go to the meeting and carry on from there, or put the prospect on your KIT list.

The advantage of this pattern is that it will give you a structure for your approaches and will start to develop your relationship marketing programme, but without antagonizing the person you are trying to reach.

Implementation plans

Plans which are put together once a year and never revised are not plans: they are archive documents. Marketing plans should be living, organic programmes. Ideally, they should be prepared on a 13-month rolling basis, and updated every

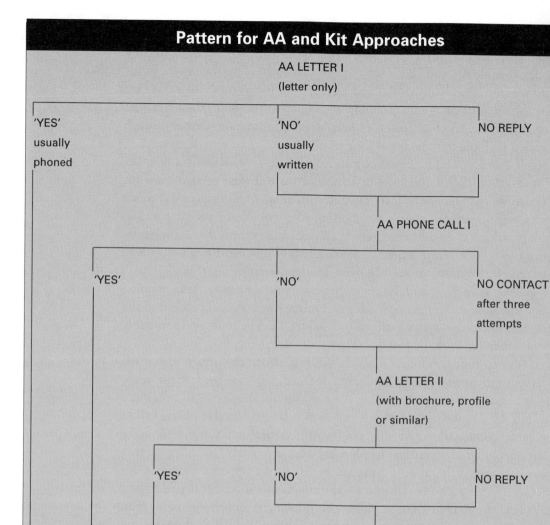

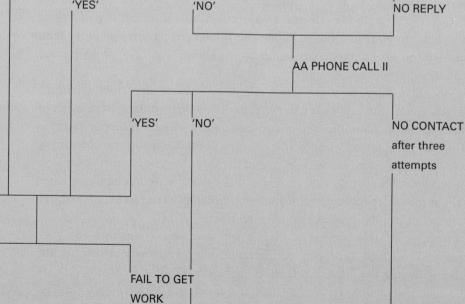

Pattern for AA and Kit Approaches

AA LETTER I
(letter only)

'YES'
usually
phoned

'NO'
usually
written

NO REPLY

AA PHONE CALL I

'YES'

'NO'

NO CONTACT
after three
attempts

AA LETTER II
(with brochure, profile
or similar)

'YES'

'NO'

NO REPLY

AA PHONE CALL II

'YES' 'NO'

NO CONTACT
after three
attempts

GET
WORK

FAIL TO GET
WORK

KIT PROGRAMME

month to take account of changing developments in the marketplace, tactical opportunities and your own circumstances. The specific content of your plan will depend, of course, on your objectives, and on how many different target market sectors you have identified; you might need to do a separate plan for each. It will also depend on your available budget and other resources such as time and people.

Good plans should contain details of what is to be done, when it is to be done, who is to do it, and how much each activity will cost.

A simple example for a medium-sized, established design company is shown on p. 76 and on p. 77 there is an example for a small, newly launched design company.

If you plan in this way, you will avoid one significant problem which most design companies, particularly the smaller ones, encounter: when you are busy with ongoing work, you have no time for marketing. Once you stop being busy, it is too late to do your marketing in time to fill the gap, and a 'peaks and troughs' pattern of work emerges. By spreading the marketing activities in a planned manner across the year, you can help to even out the workload.

Activity 8

This activity is designed to start you thinking about your implementation plan.

A Think about integrated marketing. Select one of your target market sectors and consider which combination of broadshot and bullseye approaches would be the most appropriate. Try to allocate a percentage of importance to each, so that you begin to plan the relative weight you intend to put behind each kind of approach.

B Using the AA and KIT pattern from this chapter as a model, take three examples of people you have approached over the last 12 months or so and, for each one, track the progress of your phone calls and written communications to them during that time. Did they follow a logical pattern? Were your communications regular and consistent? Did the approaches result in actual work? Learn from what you have done in the past and try to develop a workable pattern for the future.

C Draft a marketing plan for the next 13 months for your company, based on:
- your desired target market sectors (remembering that you might need to do one for each if they are very different)
- your company's available people, time, skills and budget resources.

Implementation Plan for a Medium-sized, Established Design Company

MONTH	ACTIVITY	WHO	COST (£)
September	Press campaign launch of new WonderGlobe work	Maria and Glory Glory PR	2 500
	Create WonderGlobe mailer	Robby	1 000
	Autumn training seminars clients and hot prospects	Louis and Training for Clients Ltd	4 000
October	KIT mailing whole databank – WonderGlobe	Jean-Luc	500
	AA letters and phone calls, food retailers (continues to end December)	Sarah	300
November	10th anniversary party for clients, hot prospects, media and key suppliers	Maria and Glory Glory PR	2 000–2 500
December	New Year cards and limited edition seasonal gifts	Helmut	1 000
January	AA letters and phone calls, airlines (continues until end March)	Sarah	300
	Press campaign launch of new Unibixx work	Maria and Glory Glory PR	2 500
	Create Unibixx mailer	Robby	1 000
February	KIT mailing whole databank – Unibixx mailer plus press articles	Jean-Luc	500
March	Spring training seminars clients and hot prospects	Louis and Training for Clients Ltd	4 000
April	USA Works exhibition Colorado (to be confirmed)	Matt and Sophie	8 000–10 000
	AA letters and phone calls, healthcare (continues until end June)	Sarah	300
May	Press campaign launch of new MegaUtility work	Maria and Glory Glory PR	2 500
June	KIT mailing whole databank – MegaUtility mailer plus press articles	Jean-Luc	500
July	AA letters and phone calls, government (continues until end August)	Sarah	300
August	Review results, set budgets for next year	Team	–
September	AA letters and phone calls, telecommunica-ions (continues to end December)	Sarah	300
	Press campaign launch of new work ??what	Maria and Glory, Glory PR	2 500
	Create mailer ??what	Robby	1 000
	Autumn training seminars clients and hot prospects	Louis and Training for Clients Ltd	4 000

Implementation Plan for a Small, Newly Launched Design Company

MONTH	ACTIVITY	WHO	COST (£)
September	Develop letter plus photo print of CombiMed work	John	100
October	KIT mailing whole databank – CombiMed	John	60
	AA letters and phone calls, grocery (continues to end December)	John	30
November	1st anniversary party	Suzie	250
December	and joint Christmas party for clients, hot prospects, media and key suppliers		
	Christmas cards	Suzie	150
January	AA letters and phone calls, financial (continues until end March)	John	30
	Create WhizziCo letter plus photo prints	John	100
February	KIT mailing whole databank – WhizziCo	John	60
March	Easter egg gift for clients, hot prospects and media	Suzie	150
April	AA letters and phone calls, airlines (continues until end June)	John	30
May	Press campaign launch of new WonderCo work	Suzie	–
	Create WonderCo letter plus photo prints	John	100
June	KIT mailing whole databank – WonderCo (plus press articles)	John	60
July	AA letters and phone calls, transport (continues until end September)	John	30
August	Review results, set budgets for next year	Both	–
	Consider creation of a company brochure	Both	–
September	Press campaign launch of new work ??what	Suzie	??
	Create mailer ??what	John	??

9 WORDS AND PICTURES: IT'S BOTH WHAT YOU SAY AND THE WAY YOU SAY IT

'Thunder is good, thunder is impressive, but it is the lightning that does the work.'
Mark Twain: *Letters* August 28 1908

■ Sales letters
■ Mailers and profiles
■ Brochures

Sales letters

For most design consultancies, a mailing campaign should start with a letter alone, without mailers, profiles, brochures or other enclosures. The best way to penetrate directly into a potential client's mind at the AA phase is to write a professional, business-to-business letter whose contents are pertinent to the prospect individual's current commercial needs. That is not to say that mailers, or mailshots as they are sometimes called, are not useful: they have an important role which will be discussed in the next section. However, mailers are by their very nature less personal. Are you going to produce an item solely for one prospect? I doubt it, and so will they.

Equally, if on the first AA phase of your bullseye approach you send a mail-merged letter – that is one which is personalized in the sense that it is addressed to an individual, but is otherwise clearly one of several dozens or even hundreds run off your computer printer – it runs the risk of being easily discarded by the very person you most want to read it.

If, on the other hand, you can send something which is hard to ignore, and contains content of genuine interest to the person you want to build a relationship with, you stand a greater chance of success. In practice, most of us only throw away things which are easy to throw away; the rest we hoard in piles on our desks 'to attend to later'. It does not mean that we are positively inclined towards the material in question, or even that we intend to act on it; simply that we are not ready to throw it away yet. If you reach this point, at least you have cleared the first hurdle. How much better, though, to make your letter so pertinent and persuasive that you get an immediate, positive response.

Effective sales letters should be:

1 Personal

This means more than just addressing your letter to a named individual. You should aim to include content which makes it clear that you have thought about that individual's company, products and marketplace, either through past experience of that market sector, through general knowledge or through specific research. Remember how you feel when you get letters from people who clearly have no knowledge of how the design industry works. Those are the ones which are easy to put straight in the bin.

2 Relevant

If your offer – and in this case it would be an offer to meet for a short discussion to see whether you might be of help to them – is not relevant to the individual, either immediately or in the near future, your approach will fail, no matter how attractive it might be. You should aim to make a reader sit up and take notice in the opening sentences, so that they want to read on, and then provide information which is pertinent to them in their work. It might help to think of it as 'news and views they can use'. You then need to make them want to know more and, lastly, you need to let them know what they have to do next if they want to proceed. This process was formalized many years ago by the direct marketing industry into a simple system which has the mnemonic AIDA: Attention, Interest, Desire, Action. Having got a reader's Attention, you supply relevant information which will retain their Interest, create Desire to know more about whatever you are selling by putting meaningful propositions to them, and then tell them clearly what Action they will need to take if they want to take things further. It is still an excellent way of thinking about sales letters, and it can also be applied successfully to mailers, brochures and advertisements.

3 Outward-facing

Your letter must focus on the person you are writing to, not on yourself: in this way, you will automatically include sales benefits for, not features of, your company. One of the most basic principles of sales success is to concentrate on the other person's needs, desires, hopes, fears, beliefs, problems, opportunities and not on yourself. If you focus on yourself and your features, what's in it for them? You also need to make it easy for the other person to agree to your suggestion, to make it easy for them to say 'Yes'. Any hint of difficulty – including a possible need to fend off future tiresome telephone calls from you – and you will find yourself on a direct route to failure.

4 Polite

Isn't it surprising how insulting some sales letters can be? In the first place, the writer assumes that you want to know all about their company or products: 'I feel sure that you will want to benefit from our offer/expertise etc' (subtext: 'If you don't, you are an idiot'). They state that you know nothing of the subject matter in question. 'You may not realize that …' (subtext: 'You are clearly not doing your job properly'). They patronizingly beg 'A few minutes of your precious time, O busy executive' (subtext: 'If I flatter you into thinking you are a world-class leader you might give me your attention'). Moreover, if you appear too pushy, you will quickly offend. Sentences like: 'I will telephone you in a few days to arrange a meeting' are like a red rag to a bull, and can trigger the classic knee-jerk response of: 'Oh, no, you won't …'

On the tricky question of whether to use the prospect's surname, first name only or full name after the 'Dear…' in a salesletter, it can be helpful to follow a simple rule of using the formal 'Mr, Mrs or Ms Brown' until you have either been introduced to them, or spoken to them for a reasonable length of time on the telephone. Use your own first and last names to introduce yourself in person, on the phone, and in writing. 'Mr or Mrs X' sounds too distant, as though you were booking your car in for a service; a first name alone can sound too casual. When addressing other people it is difficult to offend by being too formal, and some people really object to the immediate use of their first name by complete strangers. Avoid the use of the prospect's full name in sales letters, as in 'Dear William Brown', as it creates an unnatural, distant form of language. Worse, to some people it suggests a poorly educated writer.

Getting the right tone of voice is not difficult. If you assume that the person you are writing to is perfectly intelligent and capable of doing their job, and would genuinely benefit from getting to know you and your company, you won't go far wrong. A good technique to try when composing sales letters is to imagine writing to a current, respected client, that is to somebody you already know quite well. Try to have an image of them sitting at their desk, reading your letter when it arrives. How might they feel? Would the content persuade them? Have you managed to use an appropriate tone of voice? If you can, ask that client to comment on your final draft letter: they will soon tell you whether you are striking the right chords or not.

The style of sales letters has changed over the years. It is no longer enough to write this sort of letter:

Mr William Brown
Brand Manager
Much Tippling Wine and Spirits
Anytown
Anywhere

Anydate

Dear Mr Brown

As a brand manager working in the wines and spirits market, I feel sure that you will be interested in our services. We are a design consultancy specializing in packaging, sales literature, industrial and consumer products and interiors. We have been established for eight years, and are experienced in the alcoholic drinks market, with clients such as Hic Haec Hoc, Cheers Medears Beers and Worldwide Winning Wines For A Warm Winter Ltd.

If you feel that there would be any benefit in our meeting, I would be happy to welcome you to our offices, or join you at yours. I enclose a brochure which will give you an idea of some of the work we have done, and I will phone you in a few days to see whether you would like to meet.

Yours sincerely

Brandy Beaujolais
Marketing Director

Did you spot the features? More importantly, however, this kind of letter fails to connect. If Mr Brown can stop yawning for long enough, I suspect that he might put the letter and the brochure, after a cursory glance, in the bin. Why should he spend any more time on it?

A more focused approach which would certainly connect, on the other hand, would be a letter like this, which would be sent without an accompanying brochure:

Mr William Brown
Brand Manager
Much Tippling Wine and Spirits
Anytown
Anywhere

Anydate

Dear Mr Brown

82

I have been prompted to write to you by the recent introduction of the European legislation EU1234 (amendment 77) which, as you know, affects the marketing of all wines and spirits by restricting the colour palette for all packaging, sales literature, products and retail locations to yellow, white and black.

Design for the drinks sector is one of our specialist business areas, and I wondered if we could help you to protect your leading position in the market by working with you to meet the imminent legal requirements?

We have a strong team of graphic, interior and product designers in our company, and we are already developing many innovative and inexpensive solutions to the challenges created by these colour restrictions. We have worked for many years with other companies in your market, particularly Hic Haec Hoc, Cheers Medears Beers and Worldwide Winning Wines For A Warm Winter Ltd, for whom we produced the award-winning designs for the Simply Smashing chain of wine bars.

If you feel that a short meeting would be useful, I would be very happy to join you at Much Tippling in Anytown or, if you prefer, welcome you to our own offices in Boozeville.

Yours sincerely

Brandy Beaujolais
Marketing Director

You will have noticed, I am sure, that the first letter says that Brandy Beaujolais will phone Mr Brown, while the second suggests that he phones her if he is interested. The first is a threat, and will increase the likelihood of Mr Brown pulling up the drawbridge. The second is an invitation to Mr Brown to take some optional action. The net result, however, will be identical: Brandy will phone in any case in three days' time to see if Mr Brown would like to meet.

Mailers and profiles

Mailers and short profiles about your company can be used in either the AA or the KIT phases of a bullseye approach. In an AA phase, they can be used like mini-brochures, to give a brief introduction to your company and work. Their objective is to provide a means of encapsulating information about your company without having to send full, expensive brochures to people who might possibly put them straight in the waste bin. Alternatively, mailers can be used in much the same way as inventive invitations and unusual greetings cards. Here, they display your company's creative talents and give an indication of its personality; they are attention-grabbers, and their objective is to make a potential client want to find out more about you, by presenting them with something distinctive and memorable.

Depending on your company's positioning and proposition, they can be either useful door-openers or inappropriate mistakes. A printed profile is useful for most companies: to be able to hand a brief summary of your work to a large number of people can be a very cost-effective means of getting your message across. Other mailers need a greater level of thought. For example, a young, fun, packaging design consultancy targeting its services at young, fun marketing and brand managers, might be very successful with, say, some printed information sent in a can, bottle or box. A multimedia design specialist might usefully produce an exciting mailer on disk. On the other hand, a mature corporate identity or interiors or industrial design consultancy might do a great deal better with a straightforward, business-to-business letter.

All AA phase mailers and profiles should:
- Have clear objectives: what exactly are you trying to achieve?
- Be attractive, visible and memorable, but also appropriate to both your consultancy and to the potential client.
- Be consistent with your overall identity, although much more dramatic than most expressions of it. This is particularly important for profiles or mini-brochures.
- Have a clear response mechanism: how should the prospect get in touch with you? Phone? Response card?

In the KIT phase, a wide variety of mailers can be used. Here, the objective is to reinforce the relationship you have already started to develop with a potential client. The items sent will be very different from an attention-grabbing AA mailer. This is where regularly produced things such as newsletters, information about completed projects or collections of press reports come in. As we have seen previously, the ideal pattern is to send something to all potential clients on your KIT database – whatever that something might be – at least every three months, as part of a drip campaign.

All KIT mailers should:
- Be clearly part of a series, through their visual style and verbal tone of voice: if you produce one unrelated item after another, you are in danger of diluting your programme.
- Be attractive enough to keep, but inexpensive enough for your budgets should they be thrown away.

Brochures

Do you need to have a brochure? I'm afraid that the answer these days is a resounding 'Yes'. It is true that many design companies have survived for years without any method of showing their work other than in face-to-face meetings. However, times are changing. As we have already discussed, potential clients increasingly have less and less time for non-essential meetings, and although most say that they enjoy sitting down to discuss design and to see what the rest of the market is up to, they also try to protect their time as much as they can. If a prospect is resistant to a meeting, a brochure will allow you to penetrate the defences on the second written stage of an AA phase (see previous chapter), that is after the initial letter and the first round of phone calls.

The second reason for having a brochure is that if you should succeed in arranging a credentials meeting, you will need to have some way of reminding the other person or people about the work you have just been discussing. It is striking how little potential clients can remember about a design consultancy's presentation an hour or so after it is over especially if, as is often the case, several design companies are seen in the same day. Even if they make notes, it is hard for them to remember any details of the work, and the assessment conversations afterwards can often be reduced to discussions of whether it was consultancy A or B or C which had done that work for Coca Cola, or Apple or BMW and which consultancy employed that bright young man in the green jacket who spoke about the importance of accountability.

If you can afford a 60-page, full-colour brochure (these are often thinly disguised as 'books'), and you are confident that it will impress people in your chosen target market sector(s) rather than deter them by appearing too lavish and wasteful, then do it. However, a brochure does not have to be an expensive, glossy affair. What you choose to do will depend entirely on your budget and your need. The simplest brochures – and they can be extremely effective – are short desktop published (DTP) documents, with mono text and colour-scanned or laser-copied pictures of work, produced to order from your own resources, or easily purchased from elsewhere. In essence, they are business documents, but with a little imagination and interesting covers and binding devices, they can be made to look stunning.

The ideal design company brochure should:

1 Contain very clear information on (a) what you do, or the results you achieve through your work, (b) how you do it, or the methods and processes you use, and (c) for whom you do it. It is surprising how obscure some design company brochures can be. Client company names should be listed in alphabetical order (otherwise the reader will assume that you have arranged them in order of importance, or of magnitude of expenditure), and it can be helpful to indicate your clients' parent companies if they are better known. As was discussed in Chapter 3, clients are reassured if similar or otherwise respected companies have commissioned you to work for them. It is also helpful to state how long you have worked for each client, as evidence of repeat business is always an indication of your clients' satisfaction.

2 Be distinctive and memorable in appearance. Some companies make their brochures larger than normal, but be careful: if you make it too difficult to file or keep in the usual places, your strategy might prove counter-productive and

your brochure might be thrown away for that reason alone.

3 Be visually and verbally consistent with the rest of your marketing material. A brochure should not be used as an opportunity to do something different for a change just because you have become bored with the look of things. If you are that bored, change your whole identity.

4 Use minimum text. Most clients have neither the time nor the inclination to read essays on design and its purpose. Your proposition or, in other words, why they should bother appointing you, should be clearly but subtly introduced.

5 Wherever possible, show before and after photographs, clearly identified – it is not always obvious. If the 'before' work is also yours, so much the better: it proves that you are not afraid of change, and that you keep your clients.

6 Show your work in a large format; you need a magnifying glass to see some design consultancies' work as shown in their sales material. Are they ashamed of it? Any particularly interesting details should be blown up even larger if appropriate.

7 Give sales and/or research results wherever available; the effect of the design in the marketplace is much more significant to most clients than the overall aesthetic nature of the work.

8 Have client quotes on how the designs were received as additions to or replacements for hard market data. Most clients are happy to supply quotes: some even ask their design companies to draft one for them.

9 Mention any creative and effectiveness awards won for the work. Both are valid.

10 Be designed in such a way that it can easily be updated without having to reprint the whole thing, or discard large cupboardfuls once the original is out of date.

Whether the printed medium, or some of the slightly newer communication methods such as video or multimedia, is best for your brochure will depend on your product, your positioning and your target market. Video and multimedia formats in disk, CD-ROM or on-line versions can provide very useful and dramatic additional support channels for your communication programmes. However, they have not yet replaced the printed medium, largely because of the relatively poor ease of access potential clients still have to the hardware necessary to view video or digital material; often, they have to book a conference room at work to view it, or take the item home with them. Finally, if you are thinking of producing hi-tech sales materials, do make sure that you have the budget to do it properly. Badly produced materials will be off-putting to all but the most devoted cyber-fan.

Activity 9

This activity will teach you to improve your analytical skills when reviewing your own letters, brochures, profiles and mailers.

A Write a sales letter to one of your existing clients, as though they were a new prospect. Try to follow the AIDA system (Attention, Interest, Desire, Action). Make sure that it is personal, relevant, outward-facing and polite. If you have a good enough relationship with that client, show your letter to them, and ask them how they would react if they received it from a different design company. What would they do as a result?

B We usually note only the general content of sales letters before deciding to put them in either the waste bin or a pile of things to read later. We do not usually spend time studying the structure and the style. Ask your colleagues to pass on to you any sales letters they receive, and study them carefully.

- How accurate are the name and address details?
- How do you feel about the content?
- Which did you find convincing, and why?
- Which failed to work, and why?

C Collect together mailers and profiles that are sent to you by other companies and make sure your colleagues do the same. Then run a discussion session where you all analyse the items. Which are effective? Why? Some of them will have been produced by leading direct response agencies for their clients, who will have paid good fees for the work: learn from them.

D If you already have a brochure, use the ten-point guidelines in this chapter to see how it performs. Also, collect other companies' brochures and analyse them with your colleagues, in the same way as you will have done with mailers.

10 RESOURCES: MAN AND MACHINE

'Measure what can be measured, and make measurable what cannot be measured.'
Galileo Galilei

- People power
- Areas of expertise
- People management
- Database development
- Sources of information
- Cleaning and validating
- Money matters

People power

Who should develop and carry out your marketing programme? Should it be done entirely from your own internal resources? If so, who exactly should be responsible? Or should you employ external consultants and specialists? Depending on your available skills, time and financial resources, you might decide to use a mixture of internal and external help.

However, whether you are a multi-disciplinary design consultancy with a hundred members of staff, or a partnership of two, the starting point will always be the same. Unless you work alone, in which case there is only one option, you must nominate one person to have overall responsibility for your marketing programme. This person must be (a) senior enough to have both authority and the ability to take decisions, often very quickly, (b) a full-time member of staff, (c) in a position to have an overview of all of the company's marketing activities, and (d) able to reconcile budgets. This person will not necessarily do all of the marketing work on their own: the various tasks can be shared by external specialists, if used, and by as many other members of the company as appropriate. However, the reporting structure and the centralization of responsibility must be clearly defined as shown in the chart.

For example, junior members of the team can manage the database or organize invitations to training sessions or events, leaving senior people free to do the things only they should do, such as making direct approaches by phone or letter,

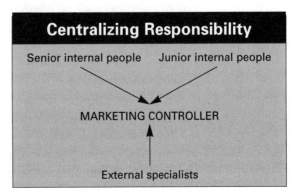

Centralizing Responsibility

Senior internal people   Junior internal people

MARKETING CONTROLLER

External specialists

networking and attending credentials presentations. A mistake frequently made by design consultancies is to allow these critical tasks to be carried out by staff who are not the equivalent, or higher, level of seniority to the prospective client. Junior people can sell water-cooling devices for offices – just. They cannot, and should not attempt to, sell professional, business-to-business services. Having said that, it is the equivalent level which is the important criterion, rather than absolute seniority: a 22-year-old might relate very successfully to a young brand manager of the same age. So might an experienced 50-year-old, who will be able to offer help and advice to the prospect. However, only the most exceptional 22-year-old could convince the chairman of a large plc with any ease.

If you work in a large enough consultancy, it makes sense to employ a full-time marketing person or people. Ideally, he, she or they should be responsible only for marketing and sales to new potential clients. As soon as a design consultancy's marketing director, manager or executive becomes involved with ongoing project work for existing clients, the new business priorities slip down to the bottom of the pile. Why? Is it because project work is more exciting, more rewarding? No: it is because the old law of 'it's the squeaky wheel which gets the grease' comes into play. If a current client wants something done, it immediately takes precedence over, say, devoting time to a telephone campaign or writing a press release.

In smaller consultancies, of course, everyone has to turn a hand to a variety of activities, and a dedicated marketing person would be a luxury few could afford. In a one-man band, of course, you turn a hand to everything. Here, good time management becomes a useful ally. A disciplined division of time to be allocated to new and existing business, plus help from productive and effective systems, will help to make sure that the marketing tasks do not get forgotten.

Why use external consultants? Firstly, they have different craft skills from yours, and are experts in their fields; they do not have to learn the hard way. Secondly, they can be very objective about your business. Thirdly, if you are paying them to do a job, they will do it; no excuses about client work getting in the way. Lastly, they can be more cost effective; you are paying for a known quality and quantity. None of the hours you put into a marketing programme is recoverable against current project client work. If you estimate the number of man hours required, and then ask yourself whether it is better for you to (a) spend that time yourself out of overheads, or (b) spend a certain amount of money for someone else's equivalent time, while spending your own time earning money from chargeable client work, then the answer will be obvious. The important thing is to use external consultants for the right tasks, and not for tasks which you could cover better, or more cheaply, in-house.

Areas of expertise

What will you need in terms of expertise if you use external consultants? The three prime areas are strategic development, PR and telemarketing.

1 Strategic development

A strategic marketing consultant will be able to help you to sort out your objectives, positioning, target markets, sales propositions and approach methods.

They will also be able to advise on the content of promotional material such as letters and brochures, and can often organize or provide training in telephone and face-to-face sales techniques, presentation skills and negotiation skills. They might work with you on the development of an improved database, and will be able to recommend external suppliers of, say, PR consultancy or telephone marketing. On the whole, they will not actually carry out your marketing programme for you. Instead, they will set it up so that you run it yourself, and so that you can continue to run it once you leave their protective wing.

There is a very small number of independent marketing consultants working exclusively in the design sector. A slightly larger group works within the wider communications or creative services sectors, and would include, for example, advertising agencies, PR companies or sales promotion companies in their client portfolios. By far the largest group of consultants offering strategic development advice is that containing marketing generalists, who might work for a diversity of companies ranging from sausage manufacturing to the shoe industry. Each has their merits. A specialist will already have a profound knowledge of the design business and how it operates: a generalist will need a longer learning curve, but ideas which have worked for other industries might prove to be useful. All of them will charge a daily rate, which will almost certainly be lower than yours and, on receipt of a brief, all will be able to give you a proposal or terms of reference for a programme, complete with an estimate of costs, before you commit yourself to further action.

2 PR consultants

If you are thinking of employing an external PR company or individual, the important thing is to be clear on your objectives, and give them free access to information and people. Again, there are design specialists and market generalists. On the whole, the specialists are preferable, as they not only know the design sector well but also have contacts in the right places; a PR expert in marine biology might have unparalleled craft skills, but will need to learn about the design business from the beginning.

Only the largest companies can afford to employ, or indeed have the need for, a full-time internal PR person; most have someone working with them for as much time as necessary, which might range from a day a month to three days a week. If not a full- or part-time member of staff, PR consultants will charge a daily rate, and will either work on a set project (eg to organize and promote a significant anniversary event) or work on a retained basis, with a contract.

PR people do much more than write press releases. They organize events for the company and its clients, they make sure that their directors are on the list of potential speakers at conferences, they ghost-write speeches, articles, letters and brochures, they develop PR-worthy research projects. They generally make things happen. Behind almost every successful design guru, there is a hard-working (but invisible) PR professional.

3 Telemarketing

The choice of available services in the telemarketing business is bewildering, as is the range of companies providing them. There are a few specialist companies working in the creative services field but, at the time of writing, none working exclusively in the design sector. These tend to be smaller companies, and there is an argument for employing a telemarketing company to be an extension of your own, rather than sub-contracting the whole job to a faceless army. Again, you will need to be very clear about your objectives. Remember that you will need outbound services, not inbound; you will be able to deal with enquiries yourself.

Most companies will work with your own database, or will develop one for you by obtaining suitable lists; they might even have an appropriate one to sell to you. Others will insist that you work with theirs. With the first, you will have a database at the end of the programme; with the second, you will not.

Telemarketing companies charge for their services in two different ways. The first is charging by results or so much paid per credentials meeting arranged within a specified target market. The cost will depend not only on the particular supplier's rates, but also on the perceived difficulty of making the appointment. A meeting with a purchaser of, say, information or marketing brochures is fairly easy to arrange: there is a huge number of potential buyers who make relatively frequent purchases. Conversely, a meeting with the chairman of a top 1000 company might take a little longer to fix. The second charging method is by number of phone calls made, regardless of whether they achieve a result. Although the first method might seem on the face of it to be more attractive, the second can be more cost effective, as each call made will promote your company, and will give you the opportunity to send a brochure, and to put the prospect's details – now qualified, or researched – on to your database.

Other areas of expertise which will be required are (i) database management and (ii) the ability to make successful credentials presentations and pitches. In my view, these tasks should be undertaken in-house. Only you can keep an accurate track on all contacts with potential clients. Only you can provide the best information in the most persuasive manner in a sales meeting. Only you can sell your creative solutions. Please see the comments on databases later in this chapter, and suggestions for presentations and pitches in Chapter 11.

People management

Whether you choose to employ external strategic or tactical consultants, or elect to do everything in-house, there are some basic guidelines for people management which will help you to achieve the results you want.

Firstly, set goals for what is to be achieved. The most basic of these will be a written job description. What does the work entail? What is expected? Most successful design companies have written job descriptions for every one of their staff. However, you might like to also consider job descriptions for any external consultants employed on an ongoing basis.

Having looked at the overall goals, the next stage is to set objectives for each task or project. As we saw in Chapter 2, all goals, or objectives, must be challenging, realistic in terms of the resources provided, specifically worded, clearly understood and agreed by everyone concerned, time-defined, measurable and frequently revised. In this situation, they must also be achievable through marketing activities;

'to increase our profit by 20 per cent by the end of the next financial year' is an admirable objective, but it is not a marketing objective. It cannot be achieved through marketing alone.

If you want to get people's commitment to a programme or course of activity, by far the best way is to ask them to set their own targets or goals: it is very likely that these will exceed any expectations you might have had. If people set their own targets, they cannot then say that they were imposed on them by a boss or client.

Secondly, make sure that the assessment criteria that you intend using are clear, and that the evaluation periods are known. Who is going to decide what is working? How often? For most design consultancies, a formal review of progress once a month is sufficient. However, you will also need feedback from the people in charge of front-line communications. What is happening? What successes have been achieved? How? What failures have there been? Why? What can you learn from both success and failure?

Thirdly, try to give constructive feedback to everyone on the team, in order to motivate them. This does not mean looking at the world through rose-tinted spectacles. It does mean using opportunities to give praise or criticism effectively. In fact, praise given badly can be almost as damaging as a resounding telling-off. How can this be? Think about the way we learn to do anything, from childhood upwards: we imitate or listen to instructions, we experiment, and we learn from our successes and failures. Unless we receive a firm 'No!' from time to time, we assume that our behaviour, or actions, have been acceptable. We do not need praise to reinforce this belief, merely the lack of criticism. There is a phrase which sums it up: 'Silence will be deemed to be tacit consent.' If, on the other hand, we receive praise – however offhand or faint-hearted – for something, especially for results which we know were mediocre, we repeat that behaviour or action. Moreover, if you dish out praise to everyone all of the time in an effort to be liked or in a misguided attempt to win loyalty or motivation, your praise will soon become valueless. Who needs praise from someone to whom it is as automatic as breathing? Any praise given should:

- Be as close to the event as is realistic; usually, you want the behaviour to be repeated in the near future.
- Specifically refer to one or more actions or results; generic praise is nice to hear but useless in its effect, as we all need to know what exactly it was that we did that was so good.
- Be given in public wherever possible, or repeated in public where it is not possible first time around; public praise adds value to the message, and will encourage the others to want to have some too.
- Be personal to one or more people, who should be mentioned by name; praise given to those who do not deserve it will only irritate and cause resentment among those to whom it belongs by right.

Any criticism given should be clear and direct. The more powerful it is, the greater its effect will be. However, badly given criticism can destroy an otherwise good working relationship. If you want to avoid alienating and demotivating any erring members of your marketing team, your criticism must also:

- Be as close to the event as is realistic, but never in genuine anger. Express anger by all means to drive the point home, but if you are genuinely upset, you are likely to exaggerate the behaviour in question, you might say something you later regret. You will be seen by the other person as an out-of-control bundle of aggression: all they will see is anger, not the reason for it, and they will become defensive. They will also lose respect for you as a result.
- Specifically refer to one or more actions or results. Be clear: exactly what did the other person do wrong? You are trying to stop them doing it again.
- Be given in private, always. If you criticize someone in public – in other words in someone else's hearing – you run several risks. Of course, it is more embarrassing for the person you are criticizing, but it is also possible that you are wrong in your accusations; privacy allows both parties to sort out the details. In addition, if you criticize someone in public, everyone else present will automatically feel sorry for the person criticized, even if they know that the person concerned is in the wrong. You need the team on your side, not against you.
- Criticize the behaviour or action, not the person. If you say: 'You are useless – you can't even proof read a simple mailer', the result will be a defensive denial. If, on the other hand, you say: 'You failed to proof read the mailer accurately, and this means that we will have to reprint them', you can both examine this unacceptable behaviour more dispassionately, and work out a way to avoid it happening again.

Finally, communicate. Listen to and learn from all of the members of your in-house team, and let them listen to and learn from you and each other. If you are using a mixture of in-house staff and external consultants, make sure they all know what is going on in your company, and what each other is doing. This is where a regular new business meeting with all interested parties can help. Weekly written status reports from all parties are also essential and should be distributed to the whole team. Good communication will ensure, for example, that an external PR consultant knows which newsworthy work is coming up, and it will encourage telemarketing staff and suppliers to keep a broader picture in mind when speaking to potential clients. It also makes sure that the marketing controller is fully aware of everything going on and can give directions to avoid omission or duplication.

Database development

At its simplest, a database is just a collection of information, organized in an accessible and usable form. It could be on sheets of loose paper, on index cards or in a bound book. For example, a standard address book is a database once it has got a number of names, addresses and phone numbers listed in it in alphabetical order. However, although many design companies have used a variety of database storage and retrieval systems ranging from loose-leaf binders to sets of index card boxes, you cannot beat a good computer system.

The trouble with non-computerized methods is not the input of data (that's just about the same whether you type it on to a screen or write it on a card). Nor is it the storage (although if you are managing a very large database, it will certainly take up less office space if you store on disk rather than on paper or card). The problem lies in its management at the use and output end. Ring binders simply do not have facilities such as an automatic name search, easy updating without illegible handwritten notes, cross-referencing, sorting or printing mail-merged letters and labels.

You do not need anything fancy or expensive in terms of software, and you will not need hardware powerful enough to run Amsterdam Schiphol Airport's air traffic control. What you will need from a computerized database, on which you can get the best advice from a good computer supplier, is a system which is capable of:

1 Storing as much data as you will use; it is sensible to buy a larger capacity than you think you need.
2 Being used by as many people as need it, preferably at the same time through a local area network, and be comprehensible to all of them; there are a number of design company databases around which can only be used by the person who set it up in the first place. Having said that, it is important that one person is responsible for the overall management and control of the database, or chaos will quickly take hold.
3 Finding and retrieving the required information quickly through the use of word or name search processes.
4 Sorting data, such as by alphabetical order of company or of potential client individual name.
5 Selective retrieval, for example:
   - accessing only the names of potential client companies with a certain level of turnover
   - or in a certain geographical area
   - or with certain design needs
   - or who use only a certain design discipline
   - or by 'hot, warm or cool' likelihood of giving you any business
   - or by people not contacted for, say, the last six months
   - or by people to be written to or telephoned that week or that day as part of a KIT programme

   If your database cannot do this, you will have to have separate databases for each defined category or use elaborate and time-consuming search techniques.
6 Outputting data in a usable form, for example as mail-merged letters or address labels.
7 Handling both static data (which only changes when details of a prospect individual or company change) and dynamic data (which constantly changes as a result of your actions and their responses).

   Static data should include:
   - prospect name*
   - title (Mr, Ms etc)*
   - job title*
   - salutation (John, Mr Bloggs etc)*

- company name*
- company address*
- telephone number
- fax number
- e-mail number
- market sector company operates in
- whether direct or third party (eg PR company)
- prospect individual's job responsibilities
- types of design commissioned
- which other design companies currently used
- estimate of potential expenditure on design per year
- how details of prospect obtained (eg from a directory, client recommendation, incoming enquiry etc)

this data will be needed for mail-merge purposes

The dynamic data should include:

- status of prospect (AA or KIT)
- details of all last contact occasions
  - date
  - by whom
  - with what/how
  - result/what said
- next action to be taken
  - date
  - by whom
  - with what/how
- notes on useful information heard on the grapevine or seen in the media.

8 Cross-referencing, or relating one piece of information to another, for analysis purposes. A good database system will be able to help you with not only records but also evaluation. This will help with your future planning. How many new approaches have you made in the last year? How many converted into credentials presentations? How many into pitches or proposals? How many into actual business? On average, how many contact occasions does your company require over what period of time to reach these different points along the chain? Once you have the information, you can plan ahead accordingly or make any adjustments to your programme that seem sensible.

A simple bar chart, updated every quarter, which sets out the numbers of actions required at each of the four main contact points (approach; credentials presentation; the preparation of a written proposal or a competitive pitch; and active business) can help you to monitor progress.

Unfortunately, there is no magic formula which will tell you that a design company 'ought to' convert x per cent of its approaches to active business: every company is different. On the whole, the more specialist your offer, the higher the rate. Conversely, you will have fewer potential prospects to approach in the first place. By carefully analysing your own conversion rates, you will be able to tell:

i On average, how many approaches you are likely to need to make to get each piece of active business.

ii Where any problem areas lie: for example, if you are managing to schedule a great number of credentials presentations, but are never asked to submit proposals or to pitch, you need to find out why. If you are frequently pitching, but never seem to win those pitches, you need to address that particular area.

iii Over time, whether your conversion rate is improving or not.

Please note that if you work in the UK and store computerized data about individuals (other than their names and addresses for mailing purposes alone), you are required by law to register your interest with the Data Protection Registrar. This is simple and inexpensive. The registration applies only to data stored on computer: manual, non-computerized systems are exempt. If you are working outside the UK, it is worth checking the current situation with the appropriate body for your own country.

Sources of information

Where can you obtain information on prospective clients? You can either purchase data or assemble it yourself. Either way, you want the best quality list possible. Many direct mail experts consider that the quality of your list is more important than the quality of your letter or mailer.

If you decide to purchase information, there are two types:

1 In-depth database details on disk or hard copy

These are usually bought for a limited number of companies or market sectors, and tend to be most useful in FMCG (fast moving consumer goods) markets or for the top 1000 companies. They will give you names, titles, roles, addresses, expenditure, known suppliers and recent market or company developments – very similar, in fact, to what you would compile yourself. The data can be used over and over again, and can form the foundation of your own database. This kind of data is available from specialist suppliers of market information, details of which can usually be found from your country's main marketing body, which in the UK is the Chartered Institute of Marketing, or through direct marketing trade bodies, the chief one of which in the UK is the DMA (Direct Marketing Association), or through advertisements in the marketing trade press.

Conversion Rate

% Approaches

95

2 Names and addresses on disks, hard copy or labels

This is what you will get from list brokers, who can be found from directories or the marketing trade press, and from organizations, which often rent out lists of their members, or from publications, who will mail your material to their subscription list. You rent the list, you do not buy it outright. Usually, you can have the lists on disk, paper or labels, and you will be asked for the purpose of your mailing and the approximate date. What's to stop you using the addresses time and time again? Most of them will have a false address or two planted among them, so that the owner of the list can tell if it is being used for unauthorized purposes. There is often a lot of wastage from a rented list, as you usually cannot specify subsections of it. For example, if you rented a business magazine's list in order to reach potential clients, there is usually no way, other than editing the labels yourself, of preventing your competitors from receiving the information. This is particularly difficult with renting lists from organizations who insist on sending the information out for you: you never see the actual list.

If you decide to do it yourself, there are several sources of information:

1 Directories

Most good reference libraries have a surprisingly wide selection of business directories where you can look up the specific information you need; the range held by business libraries is often magnificent. Some colleges and universities permit use of their business school libraries. It is also worth checking what's available from your local marketing organizations: in the UK, the Institute of Directors and the Chartered Institute of Marketing have good library facilities for members.

2 Media

Get into the habit of noting any likely looking names and companies mentioned in newspapers and magazines. You will have to do further research to get their full contact details, but it can be a good starting-point.

3 In-bound enquiries

Capture any incoming enquiries for future use, remembering to find out how they learnt about you in the first place. You will note that there is a section for this information in the static section of the suggested contents for a database.

Cleaning and validating

A database which is not cleaned regularly is a health hazard. Not only will you waste time, energy and money in sending messages to the wrong person, but you run the risk of alienating the very people you are trying to impress, by sending them inaccurate information.

A clean database comprises four elements:

1 It must be accurate: the names and titles of all individuals and the name and address of their company must all be correct, and correctly spelt.

2 It must be kept up to date. The best way to do this is to make sure that someone sets time aside every six months and phones to make sure that the details are still relevant, and that your prospect has not won the Lottery and taken early retirement. If you cannot face doing it yourself, employ temporary help; it is not

expert work. However, bear in mind that with the increase in the use of direct lines and voicemail, it is possible that a telephone call designed for database cleaning purposes could be swiftly changed into a sales or KIT call if the prospect answers the phone.

3 It might need 'de-duplicating'. If you have acquired information from more than one source, a prospect might be listed two or three times. A client contact once had seven identical design company mailers in her post one morning: three had been sent to her personally, but with slightly different spellings of her surname, and four had been forwarded to her by colleagues who had rightly taken the view that she was the person who dealt with design. A de-duplicating software programme would not have prevented this happening: there are times when only a combination of manual editing plus common sense will work.

4 It is necessary to throw information out from time to time or your database will become unwieldy. Is that charming Slovakian you met at a conference ever going to give you work? Will the marketing manager who is beginning to show signs of serious irritation with your phone calls ever say yes? If in doubt, throw them out (or at least put the information into a second, archive database, just in case).

Money matters

The real power of marketing lies in the brain, not in the wallet. Imagination, consistency and persistence often turn out to be more useful assets than a cheque book. However, money helps: it means that you can do more things more quickly. Whether your annual marketing budget is small or large, there are several things you need to bear in mind when it comes to the financial administration of your planned marketing programme.

Firstly, as has already been recommended, always set financial targets in terms of fee income, or gross profit, and not turnover. Turnover is only an indication of the amount of money passing through your bank account, and the size and nature of most design companies' businesses is such that suppliers usually get paid either before or at the same time as the client pays the design company. There is usually little opportunity to invest for interest any money coming in before it is paid out again.

Secondly, in order to gauge how much additional income you will need to bring in from new client commissions, you first need to establish the fee income you know you will have from confirmed projects. For many design companies, particularly those working in graphics, it is not possible to do this with any accuracy for more than a few months ahead. Once you have an idea of your likely monthly fee income, you can assess it against the known monthly cost of running your business. Any shortfall is the amount of new business you must acquire in that month simply in order to stand still. This exercise has been known to focus the mind of many a design company, and prevent them from spending too much time chasing after particularly low-income or low-profit projects.

Thirdly, you can usefully evaluate your average cost of sales. How much did each active piece of business cost you to obtain? The toughest measure is when you include your time costs as well as your bought-in costs. This exercise is useful for forward planning and financial analysis purposes: the lower the cost of sales, the higher the profitability of your company overall.

Finally, if you employ a new business person, it will take six months at least for the results of their efforts to be felt, even if they arrive at your company with a contacts list as long as a bright summer's day. Design companies who dismiss new business staff after six months are wasting their money: the person is probably just at the point when they are beginning to get somewhere. Be prepared to make an investment in that person for at least a year.

For much more information and advice on managing the financial aspects of your marketing programme, please read David Jebb's contribution which follows this chapter.

Activity 10

A Following the marketing strategy and plan which you have developed, allocate tasks to people. Can you manage the programme effectively in-house or will you need external help? Is any external help likely to be from a specialist or do you simply need an extra pair of hands?

B Investigate the database capabilities of the hard and software you already have; if in doubt, talk to your supplier. If it is inadequate, research other applications, taking professional advice wherever necessary. Research training courses for key staff if necessary.

C Research sources of information, and form a view on their quality and associated costs. How will you go about compiling your database?

D If you already have a good database, find out when it was last cleaned and validated; 'recently' can often turn out to be two years ago.

E Using the information and advice contained in David Jebb's contribution, and basing your work on the implementation plan you have developed, start to think about:

- setting a total budget (bought-in items plus staff plus external specialists' fees) for your marketing activities
- establishing financial sales targets on a monthly basis for the year ahead
- methods of remunerating your marketing and sales staff.

On budgets and expenditure

DAVID JEBB: DAVID JEBB AND ASSOCIATES

- But is it cost effective?

Let us start with the obvious. Design consultancies, when considering the marketing effort required to win and to keep business, must always be careful to consider the financial implications of their decisions.

The principals of a consultancy need to calculate their marketing budget in advance of spending it, rather than going ahead with what they feel to be necessary, and only working out later how effective or ineffective it has been, and what it has cost. They must remember that all marketing costs will need to be met from the profit that it generates. There will usually be a period of initial investment before the marketing pays for itself, but this cannot be greatly extended and, unless marketing generates more additional profit than it costs, it will not have been worthwhile.

In the case of small single-principal consultancies, both promotion and production will be under the overall control of one individual; in such companies the principals are in effect selling themselves. The biggest single drawback to this is that one person can not both promote and produce simultaneously. Either they are producing, in which case they are not promoting effectively, or they are promoting, in which case the consultancy's production will suffer. It is at this stage that it is very tempting to become too closely allied to a single client who is able to meet your needs and with whom you have developed a good rapport. This in effect turns the sales activity of the company into an account management role, which makes life easier for the overworked principal, but which is very dangerous for the long-term health of the company. It is not a question of what you do if the relationship begins to grow ragged: it is a question of what you do when the relationship almost inevitably falls apart.

The traditional way past the promotion/production block is for the small consultancy to have two principals, with one responsible for the creative side of the business and the other for sales and marketing. To support two principals, the consultancy obviously needs to produce at a substantially higher level from day one, but if it can generate enough business to do so, its chances of long term success are substantially greater.

For larger consultancies, both marketing and its staffing need to be looked at in detail, and the costs and anticipated rewards calculated carefully. You will need to take into account:

1 the setting of expenditure budgets for marketing
2 the establishment of financial sales targets, and
3 the most effective way of remunerating sales and marketing staff.

1 Setting expenditure budgets for marketing

The biggest single item of marketing expenditure for small consultancies is not media and other promotional costs, but the employment cost of the marketing people themselves. Setting the salary element is relatively straightforward. Unless you are going to tempt a good person on board with a genuine, short-term prospect of equity participation, the consultancy will need to pay the market rate to employ somebody with a proven competency for the job. The Americans have an expression: 'The most expensive people are always the cheapest to hire.' By this they mean that, if you look beyond the absolute cost to cost-effectiveness instead, the person who commands a good salary because they are worth it will almost always be the least expensive way of getting a job done well. As the activities that a marketing person in a small consultancy might need to cover will range from new business development and the development of existing clients to account and project management, proven competency is of the utmost importance.

It is not possible to be specific as to how many people should be employed in marketing for any particular size of consultancy. This depends on the type of work being undertaken and on the number of people who, although they are not wholly involved in sales and marketing, are able to dedicate a substantial part of their time to it, either directly or in a supporting role.

A common measure of what a consultancy should pay for the total marketing activity is about 10 per cent of gross income, which is defined as 'turnover minus the cost of material rechargeables and minus the cost of employing freelance labour'. Gross income is a much better comparative measure of output than turnover, which can be made virtually meaningless through the effect of rechargeables such as print.

Staff can be defined as either chargeable or non-chargeable. Chargeable staff habitually charge out more than 25 per cent of their weekly contracted hours, and non-chargeable staff do not. In companies employing more than five people, the proportion of 'non-chargeable' staff should ideally be less than a third. Within the non-chargeable pool – most of whom will be employed as senior managers, or in sales and marketing, account direction, account management or administration – the proportion of people directly involved in sales and marketing should not fall below two thirds.

In an 18-person consultancy, for example, at least 12 out of the 18 should be chargeable. If there are six non-chargeable staff, at least four should be directly involved in sales and marketing on a full-time basis.

Three criteria to apply when you budget your marketing expenditure are:
1 That your non-chargeable employees in total should make up less than a third of your workforce,
2 That your sales and marketing people should, ideally, number not less than two thirds of your non-chargeable employees, and
3 That the gross employment cost of people dedicated to sales and marketing should be kept within the range of 10 per cent to 12.5 per cent of gross income.

2 How to set financial sales targets

Performance statistics show that the average gross income per employee within design consultancies during the 12 months to June 1995 was running at an annual rate of approximately £60 000. Some consultancies have done a lot better than this, and some substantially worse. Based on 1995 prices, the aim should be for a gross income of between £65 000 and £70 000 per permanent employee, and this should be the global figure on which to base your calculation of sales targets.

In setting sales targets:

1 Budget for gross income and not turnover
2 Start by setting the target for the company as a whole
3 Agree how much of this can be budgeted to come from existing clients, and
4 Deduct item 3 from item 2 to establish how much business needs to come from new clients.

If your consultancy's current annual gross income per employee is above £70 000 per annum (still at 1995 prices), try to improve it further. If it is below the £70 000 benchmark, you should be seeking an improvement to your current figure of at least 10 per cent year on year until it reaches that level. This would mean that the calculation for setting the sales budget for the company as a whole would be one of the following:

1 If last year's gross income per employee was less than £63 000, (90 per cent of £70 000), set your target at 'numbers employed multiplied by 110 per cent of last year's gross income per employee'
2 If last year's gross income per employee was near enough £70 000 and you want to keep with that budget figure for the coming year, set your target at 'numbers employed multiplied by £70 000', or
3 If last year's gross income per employee was £70 000 or above and you want to set higher targets for the coming year, set your target at 'numbers employed multiplied by x per cent of last year's gross income per employee figure'.

Senior management and the people responsible for looking after business from existing clients should then determine as realistically as possible, the minimum figure, the maximum figure and median figure that can be expected to be written for each of the consultancy's existing clients during the coming year. The balance that is required to be generated by new business development can then be calculated by deducting these totals from the total budget gross income for the year.

Any sales budgeting contains a substantial proportion of 'guestimation'. However, it is easier to guess what is likely to be written with existing clients than to determine the level of new business which will be won. This is why we strongly suggest that estimating your further business from existing clients over the coming 12 months is the best place to start the forecasting exercise.

For example:
18-person consultancy,
current annual gross income per employee   £57 500
Consultancy budget for next budget year
18 x (110% of £57 500) equals 18 x £63 250   £1 138 500 of gross income
Expected business from existing clients,   £740 000
built up componentially, client by client
Gross income required to come from   £398 500
'new business' (£1 138 500 – £740 000)

3 How to remunerate marketing staff

The most common form of remuneration for marketing staff remains the same as for other employees – a salary plus, in most cases, bonuses. However, this does not give the best incentive. If you are a small consultancy where the continued client servicing is carried out by a principal, and the marketing effort of the business development manager is concentrated on new business development, payment-by-results should be considered. The purpose behind this is to reward people for what they have achieved and not to pay them a flat rate for the time that they have taken to achieve it.

Payment-by-results can be in three parts:

1 A basic salary, set at about two thirds of what you regard as a fair rate for an average person in that position,
2 A bonus for every genuine pitch that the marketing individual wins (a genuine pitch being defined as a pitch for business that is awarded to somebody even if it is not awarded to you), plus
3 A bonus for any new business which actually happens, a small percentage of which should be paid when the work is authorized, with the balance given once the client has paid in full.

The component parts of this scheme can be developed in any way that you wish. Differing weight can also be given to each of the three components, depending on your own situation and what you feel will best motivate the marketer. A good system is to set payments so that the average individual should earn about 150 per cent of the basic salary. For the superstar, there should be a cap on total earnings of two times basic salary.

From the scheme outlined above, this would mean that you might:

1 Employ someone on a basic salary of £16 000
2 Intend that if their performance is average they should earn £24 000
3 Put a cap on earnings of £32 000.

Remember that the real joy of payment-by-results is that a good level of gross income has to be generated for the individual to earn well. It must be possible for him or her to be well rewarded under the scheme, but only when the consultancy has also benefited substantially.

Larger companies, where a number of people are involved in client servicing and new business development, should consider group bonus schemes rather than individual payment-by-results. It is important that such groups are encouraged to work together rather than as competing individuals. Groups should earn a moderate level of basic salary with bonuses paid for all gross income generated in excess of a budget figure, which may well be different for client servicing and new business development. Again these schemes need to be run with a cap on earnings to ensure that they cannot get out of control. The group bonus scheme is usually best paid quarterly to bring the reward as close to the period of achievement as possible, as this has proved to be the best motivator. For example, any bonus earned during the January-March quarter would be paid in April. To participate in group bonus schemes, employees would have to have started their employment before the start of the reference period, and still be employed (and not under notice) when the reference period ends.

Some examples of how such a scheme might work are outlined below. They show how the total bonus earned by the group is divided pro rata according to the different salaries earned: within the group each individual's basic salary should reflect the value to the company of his or her input.

Assume that a four-person new business development team has its basic salaries set at two thirds of the target earnings as follows:

Numbers	Target Earnings per year	Basic salary per year	Basic salary per quarter
1	£30 000	£20 000	£5000
1	£24 000	£16 000	£4000
1	£21 000	£14 000	£3500
1	£18 000	£12 000	£3000

The total basic annual salary of the bonus-earning group therefore equals £62 000 per year or £15 500 per quarter.

The base gross income targets, over which bonus will be paid, (ie sales value minus the cost of bought-in materials and freelancers) are:

January/March	£160 000
April/June	£175 000
July/September	£160 000
October/December	£180 000

The bonus equals 20 per cent of gross income generated in excess of the base target, with a cap of 100 per cent on each individual's earnings.

Example 1

During the January/March quarter the gross income written by new clients = £150 000.

Group bonus earned Nil
(The gross income is below the base of £160 000 for the quarter which has to be achieved before a bonus will be paid.)

Example 2

During the January/March quarter new business written yields a gross income of £200 000.

Group bonus earned   20% of £40 000
                                     (£200 000 written, against £160 000 base)= £8000

This will be split according to the salary earned in the quarter and the salary bill for the group as a whole, so that the individual members of the team will receive a bonus as follows:

- The £5000 per quarter person will receive:

  $\dfrac{£8000 \times £5000}{£15\,500}$ =   £2580.65

- The £4000 per quarter person will receive:

  $\dfrac{£8000 \times £4000}{£15\,500}$ =   £2064.52

- The £3500 per quarter person will receive:

  $\dfrac{£8000 \times £3500}{£15\,500}$ =   £1806.46

- The £3000 per quarter person will receive:

  $\dfrac{£8000 \times £3000}{£15\,500}$ =   £1548.39

If the bonus earned in any quarter exceeds the basic salary for an individual for that quarter, it should be capped, at a sum equal to the basic salary. For example, if an individual's basic salary was £3500, and the calculated bonus that would be earned were £3750, the bonus would be capped at 100 per cent of the basic salary, ie at £3500.

In conclusion, whichever approach you select, you will need to set expenditure budgets, establish financial targets and develop an effective way of remunerating sales and marketing staff. If you plan and cost your proposed marketing effort with as much care as possible and measure its effectiveness month on month, it is likely to be cost effective. If, on the other hand, your marketing is carried out on an ad hoc basis, without adequate forethought, and without its effectiveness being constantly measured, how will you know whether it is worthwhile or not?

David Jebb and Associates is a UK management consultancy specializing in the design sector, offering financial, IT and other commercial advice. In addition, they provide the Design Business Performance Ratios, which give quarterly information on subscribers' comparative performance in their marketplace. For further information contact David Jebb and Associates, 10 Scott Close, Market Harborough, Leicestershire LE16 7LN, UK.

11 LIFE'S A PITCH: GETTING THE BUSINESS

'Let us never negotiate out of fear, but let us never fear to negotiate.'
John F Kennedy, Inaugural address 20 January 1961

- Credentials presentations
- Preparation
- Proposals
- Terms of business
- Competitive pitches
- Free pitching

Credentials presentations

Credentials presentations are those where you meet a potential client for the first time in a focused situation (you might previously have met him or her over a drink, on a plane or at a conference), and where you attempt to interest that potential client in the benefits of becoming an actual client.

Credentials presentations are sales meetings. They are, in fact, one of the most important presentations you will ever have to make. Not only do first impressions count, but within an ongoing client/design consultancy relationship, there will be times when you will be able to say: 'After our meeting yesterday, I'm left with the terrible feeling that I didn't put over the key points of what we are trying to achieve. Can I come and see you again?' Within the sales phase of the relationship, however, it is almost impossible to do something similar. If you feel that your company's sales skills could be improved, it is worth investing in professional sales training, but make sure that the training is geared for service industries, and not for product sales. The principles and the processes are different.

It is important to remember that there are several reasons for someone asking for or agreeing to such a meeting. It is possible that they have a specific brief in mind. If they have, they might not tell you, either because the brief in question is confidential and they do not want to spread news too widely at this stage, or because they know that if they tell a series of design companies that a project is about to go live they will receive endless follow-up telephone calls in return. However, it is also possible that the prospect is simply updating his or her general knowledge about design consultancies and what they offer. They might be very happy for the moment with their current design suppliers, with no imminent brief. Lastly, some people like to learn about (a) what is going on in their own marketplace, such as new product development case stories, or (b) use ideas discussed in credentials presentations to spark off thoughts of their own. You will never know the real reason why you are sitting there, so it is essential that you treat each case as though a live project depended on it.

Preparation

The first thing to be clear about is that there is no such thing as a standard, off-the-shelf credentials presentation. You cannot expect to succeed if all you are doing is grabbing the same old 35mm slide carousel or the ring-bound folio marked 'Company Credentials' and dashing off to a meeting, presentation and brochure in one hand and taxi fare in the other. If you want to deliver the most pertinent and effective credentials presentation possible, every one you make must be tailor-made for every potential client. Why waste your time or their time by doing anything less? As is the case with many aspects of life, preparation is the key. As the old saying goes: 'Fail to prepare and you prepare to fail.'

Here's a suggestion for a step-by-step process:

1 Be very clear about why you are doing this presentation, and what you expect to get out of it. Most guidelines on presentation skills will try to tell you that this involves the setting of an objective. The trouble with preparing for a presentation – any presentation – with an objective is that objectives are entirely self-centred: you might say 'I want to tell them about our company and the work we have done for clients X, Y and Z' or 'I would like to convince them that we are the right people for the job'. As a statement of intent, they suffice. But they are sender-focused, whereas all good communication is recipient-focused.

   A better way of preparing, therefore, is to sort out the desired response you want to elicit from the other person(s). One of the best definitions of a presentation of any kind comes from David Bernstein in his book *Put it Together, Put it Across*.

   > A presentation aims to get a thought out of your head, into someone else's and thereby change that person…. What do you want the audience to think, believe, feel, do as a result of what you are saying.

   In other words, what response do you want from the other party? You need to be realistic. Ultimately, you would like a commission from the prospect, but that is not achievable after one credentials presentation alone. At the very least, you will have to submit a cost estimate and timing plan, even if you manage to avoid a full strategic proposal or a competitive pitch, paid or unpaid.

   Realistic desired responses would be (and note the use of the recipient-focused 'you' as opposed to the more distant 'them'):
   - I would like you to understand a little of what we have done for other clients, and believe that we can help you and your company, so that you invite us to tender for the work
   - As a result of our discussion, I would like you to feel confident in our work, and comfortable with us as people, so that you consider us the next time you

need a design consultancy

- I would like you to feel so inspired by our work that you ask us to come to talk to your boss about the possibility of us joining your preferred suppliers' list.

2 Do your research: find out as much as you can about the company and the situation as you can beforehand, to avoid wasting your own time and money.

Research the prospective client company. Who owns them? Who do they own? What do they do? How do they do it? Who else is doing it in their market, and how? It is important to then formulate a view, which you should express during the meeting, about them and their products/services and about their competition from a design point of view. This means that you should not only do some desk research, but also get out and see what is happening to that company in terms of its design. Do remember, however, that you are trying to sell design services, not general business consultancy. The time to suggest that their marketing plan or business management needs attention, if at all, is when you are working with clients as a part of their team, when you will also have a better-informed viewpoint.

3 Before the meeting, telephone the contact. Not only will you be able to gain useful information, but you will also start to build a certain level of rapport with the potential client. Ask who will be present in the meeting: if you are expecting to be meeting one or two people and you end up with a roomful, it will affect not only what you say, but also the way in which you say it.

Ask your contact what they are particularly interested in discussing, to avoid wasting their time. Ask whether there is anything they can tell you about the company/product/service/specific project. Ask which design companies they have used in the past to gauge the level of their experience, and whether they are planning to see other design companies at this stage. If so, which? We are often reluctant to ask questions in case we are thought to be impertinent, but in fact, we often damage our chances at this initial stage by displaying an apparent lack of interest.

4 Confirm the appointment in writing, and phone shortly before the meeting to check it is still on. If the person you have planned to see is ill, or called away to another meeting, it is quite likely that no one will have your contact details to hand. If you do not speak to the person directly, do not worry: it is also important to build rapport with a secretary or assistant. It's harder to build rapport with voicemail, but don't forget that at least you get to 'speak to the contact themselves': leave a message and contact an assistant as well if possible.

5 Decide who should give the presentation. It should be one of the principals of the company – especially if they have their name over the door – or your best presenter, if that is not the same person. In addition, one other person should attend. It is always beneficial to have two representatives of your company, regardless of whether you are meeting one person or several: if they hate one of you on sight, there is a chance that they will get on with the other. If the contact is fairly junior, senior design professionals can seem daunting, so choose your participants carefully.

6 Decide how you will show the work (slides, flip portfolios/presenters, real samples, from a brochure etc), and make sure that you will have any necessary equipment available.

7 When putting your presentation together, do not just show piece of work after piece of work. It is very, very boring. Start instead with a short description of your company and your way of working, and then use your work to support the claims you want to make about your company. In this way, you will be able to focus on the proposition you are offering, ie on the benefits, and not the features (see Chapter 6). Whether your main selling point is attention to detail, commercial awareness, design effectiveness or European experience – prove it.

Select several examples of work which demonstrate your proposition, and then follow with just one or two in-depth case histories, which are relevant to that particular company. This is where your research comes in. By the way, don't forget to explain the relevance: it's not always obvious. It is helpful to show before and after pictures (as discussed in Chapter 9): again, it is not always obvious to the uninitiated which is which, so make it clear. Demonstrate the results of your work, and make the most of your clients' brand or company names, citing parent companies if appropriate, and explaining a little about each company.

When planning the length of your presentation, it should amount to no more than a third of your total allocated time. A half-hour meeting, for example, should include a ten-minute presentation, whereas an hour should include 20 minutes, and so on. The important thing is to listen to your potential clients and their needs, not to bend their ears about how wonderful you are.

8 On the day, arrive early. Woody Allen once said in an interview 'Eighty per cent of success is showing up.' You can add a further 5 per cent by turning up early. Not only does it give you time to collect your thoughts and make yourself comfortable, but it also allows you to absorb the culture of the company a little. One designer recently mentioned a third advantage: he had perfected the art of reading reception registers upside down to see whether any of his competitors had visited the company recently.

9 Before you present anything, listen and learn. Use your research to ask appropriate questions: this stage of the meeting is vital. Firstly, you will discover the real issues facing the potential client. If you fail to listen properly at this point and start to make assumptions, you are very likely to suggest an inappropriate solution. Asking questions and giving feedback in the form of summaries of what has just been said are the only way to demonstrate active listening. In addition, if you ask questions and listen carefully to the replies, you will learn about any subject areas to be avoided in the meeting. If the other person says that he or she has heard enough about creativity to last a lifetime, it might be best to leave out what you were going to say about your 17 Design and Art Direction awards. Or if they say that the problem they have with their current design is that it lacks impact, you can highlight the attention-grabbing effect of your own work.

Remember also to allow time for questions from the potential client and discussion of any subjects they might raise; they are far more important than sticking to your own agenda. If necessary, forget your prepared presentation altogether.

10 At the end of the meeting, leave behind a document with a summary of your presentation, including visual and verbal references to the work shown, and give them a copy of your brochure, if you have one, and if it has not previously been sent. Say how much you would like to work with them and their company, and ask what the next step is likely to be. Invite them to get in touch if they need further information and, of course, thank them for their time and interest.

11 Follow up with a letter, written the next day, and telephone a week later if you have not heard from them. Again, do not damage your chances by seeming to be uninterested in whether you work with them or not.

12 If you are unsuccessful, ask why. Equally, if you are successful, ask why. Without this knowledge, how can you discover potential areas for improvement?

Proposals

Whether they are lengthy, glossy, bound tenders or a simple letter, a proposal is one of the most important pieces of documentation ever produced by a design company. This holds true for proposals submitted for a competitive pitch for a project from a new client, or those which outline the anticipated working methods on a project for an existing client. Not only do they contain details of your recommended plan of action, but they form part of the legal contract for the supply of work to your clients. In the case of a dispute, the written proposal will become a prime piece of evidence.

Proposals usually accompany a presentation, except in the case of certain written tenders. However, they should always be written to stand alone, as they will be circulated within the actual or potential client's company to people who were not present at the presentation.

Any written document reflects the professionalism of your company: a badly written document will suggest that your design work also lacks attention to detail. A proposal is often the first piece of written work which a prospective client will receive from you. If it is badly written, it may be the only piece of work they ever see.

It follows then that proposals must be accurate, comprehensive, well structured and well written, and that management time and effort must be allocated to the development of all written work leaving the company. You can, of course, reduce the effort involved by using document templates on your word processing system, which saves both executive and processing time, and which adds a common structure and style to your proposals and other formal written communications. This is particularly important for ongoing clients.

Unless it refers to a very straightforward project and takes the form of a confirmatory letter, a full competitive proposal should include the following:

- a title page
- a contents page
- an introduction to the document/purpose of document
- a summary of the background to the project
- a statement of the design objective(s)
- an indication of the actual design work required
- details of your design company
- your proposed method of working
- brief biographical details of the individuals appointed to the project (plus photographs if appropriate)
- the recommended stages of design development
- a timing schedule
- fee and cost estimates
- a summary and conclusion
- your terms of business (see next section)
- appendices:
  - a photocopy, not a paraphrase, of the original client brief
  - any technical specifications which must be followed
  - any restrictions on the design, corporate or otherwise
  - any other relevant information.

Terms of business

It is foolish to commit yourself and your company to a project or a long-term business relationship without an agreed contract describing the terms under which your skills and services will be provided. As a minimum, your company's terms of business, or conditions of contract, should include:

1 A specification of what is to be provided, and what will be gained in return; this can be done by referring to a written letter or proposal by name and by date.

2 Details of the process of your remuneration, including when invoices will be issued, your payment terms in days, weeks or months, any VAT conditions and, where appropriate, which currency will apply. This is also the place to add any special terms you might have about late payment, for example charging a percentage fee after a certain period, and any cancellation terms you might have.

3 A clear statement of the ownership of all intellectual property rights arising from the work in question, and under what circumstances they might be transferred.

4 Under which country's law any disputes will be handled; even within the UK, Scottish law differs from English law.

5 A statement that all recommendations made will be based on information supplied by a client and their staff and consultants, and that you accept no liability for recommendations given as a result of incomplete or incorrect information received.

There are times when a client will introduce their own terms of business, either in the form of a contract or a purchase order. Most of these seem restrictive at first, but often benefit the supplier. For example, their payment terms are often favourable compared with the non-contractual payment behaviour of other clients.

If you are faced with a client's terms and conditions, read them carefully and isolate any items with which you are unhappy, so that you can negotiate. Remember that in most cases a client's terms are standard, and have been drafted to include all possible events; it is quite likely that the same contract is given to all suppliers, from management consultants to stationery companies. If you are not confident in your company's negotiation skills abilities, think about professional training. Again, make sure that the courses you select are targeted at the design community, and not at industrial relations personnel or international disaster management committees.

For drawing up your own terms of business for clients and suppliers, or for negotiating over a client's standard contract, it is wise to consult a solicitor, preferably with experience in the design sector.

111

Competitive pitches

For a competitive pitch, much more preparation is needed than for a credentials presentation, and not just in terms of the work required in strategic thinking, creative solutions, cost estimates and timing plans. Obviously, you will have to research thoroughly the prospective client's company and its market; it is dangerous to rely only on their brief to you.

However, the presentation itself will also demand more time, energy and resources in its development. Rehearse, rehearse and rehearse again the presentation itself, and make sure that everyone (and pitches almost always involve more than one person from your company unless you work alone) knows exactly what they are doing. Don't forget to mention during the presentation any creative or strategic routes you have discarded in your search for the recommended solution, and state why. It can be very frustrating to see the project awarded to another design company which suggested something which you felt would not work, but against which the potential client has not heard any counter-arguments.

In the time between the brief and the presentation try to use every available opportunity to continue building rapport with the potential clients; a good hint is to think of them as actual clients throughout, in both your attitude and behaviour.

Finally, just as with credentials presentations, do remember to ask afterwards why you were successful, or why you were not. It all helps to build up your knowledge, and will indicate if there is room for improvement.

Free pitching

As we all know, some pitches are paid for by the commissioning client. Increasingly, however, pitches have become only partly paid – often a very small token payment – or completely unpaid. Designers are being asked to provide one of the most important parts of their work – the concept stage – for free. Whose fault is this? The clients?

The design industry has taught clients over the years to ask for free work. How? Firstly by doing it when asked, and secondly – and more perfidiously – by offering to do it without being asked. In a research study done by London-based design company, The Jenkins Group, among buyers of annual reports, nearly two thirds of those interviewed selected their current design companies on the basis of a free creative pitch from the shortlisted companies. Eighty per cent said that they had involved three or more design companies in the selection process: that's a lot of creative energy in total, much of it wasted. The report states:

> Overall, the research indicates that free pitching is widespread and, if anything, increasing. Companies expect it, and there is little resistance shown from design consultants – free creative work is sometimes offered without being requested by the client. The qualitative statements show that companies use the creative pitch to help hone the brief and crystallize their ideas.

Ideally, you should never give your work away for free, unless you are supporting a charity or other good cause which would benefit from your input and which cannot afford your fees. It is often argued that it is necessary to lose a few sprats in order to catch a mackerel. The trouble is that most design companies can ill afford to end up without sprats and without mackerels, the inevitable result for all but the 'winner'. Even the design company which is awarded the project loses in the end, as it will be difficult to charge realistic prices in future for the stage of work which you have hitherto been prepared to do for no payment at all. And the clients lose overall, both in the quality of the work and financially: the funding for time donated to potential client A will have to be clawed back from actual clients B, C and D – and in the future from actual client A as well.

Of course, whether you do it or not is entirely a commercial decision. If you believe that you will gain from working for nothing at an early stage, and you can afford to do it, nothing will prevent you. However if you do not want to do it, you need some ammunition.

Firstly, you can join a national or international professional organization such as the Design Business Association (DBA) or the Chartered Society of Designers (CSD) in the UK, the PDA (pan-European Brand Design Association) across Europe, and dozens of others around the world. Most organizations have a code of conduct which discourages members from free pitching, and they can provide a useful source of support and help if you are having pressure put on you.

Secondly, you can try to draw up a contract with the potential client which includes agreed payment terms, if any, or a rejection fee. It should also contain a clear statement of who owns the rights to the work if you are unsuccessful in your pitch: you do, unless otherwise assigned.

Thirdly, there is no point in using arguments against free pitching which only address the design company side of the matter. In order to convince clients, you will have to explain to them why it is not in their own best interest to ask for free creative design work. You are welcome to use any of the following arguments:

1 Design solutions which are created to win a competition are not necessarily the correct design solutions; they are simply created to please.
2 The first important stages of a design project – thinking, exploring, researching – are the foundations of good design: professional design

companies will always spend a lot of time on these stages. Design companies participating in free pitches cannot afford to do so.

3 Good design solutions are only possible when there is a close working relationship between client and designer and time to discuss a brief in full. Everything else is just guesswork.

4 The very best design solutions are only possible when the designer feels able to tell clients that they are wrong. This is almost impossible in a free-pitch situation, where the designer will not risk upsetting a client.

5 Design companies are businesses not charities: the costs of a free pitch will often be recovered by the 'winner' in later stages of the project. Unlike advertising or direct marketing companies, design consultancies earn their fees as a result of the strategic development of design solutions, and not through commission on implementation or on media expenditure.

6 Doing work for free increases design companies' overheads; this in turn increases the total design industry's charges to clients. How else can the 'losers' recover the costs?

7 The design company owns all of the rights to the material produced for the pitch, until they are formally assigned in writing to another party. If a potential client has not paid for the work, the rights will not be assigned.

8 Requests from a client for free work are a form of pressure on price. It is not always good policy to buy the cheapest available (or free) product. Design is not just about an attractive visual idea; good design solutions get results. Good design companies provide high-quality advice and service as well as those good design solutions. It is worth paying for them.

9 No professional designer can support a system which inevitably leads to lower standards and higher costs. How many clients would want such results if they took the time to think about it?

10 A system of free pitching denies clients access to the most professional design companies: ie those who refuse to free pitch.

If none of those convince anyone asking for free work, you could try showing them *Total Branding by Design* by Paul Southgate of Wickens Tutt Southgate, in which he advises clients buying and managing brand design. On the subject of free pitching he includes this comment:

> Never, never ask design companies to do free work in a pitch situation. What you will get are superficial 'concepts', done by whichever designers happened to have a bit of time on their hands. There is a chance that the perfect solution will be among them, but it is about as likely as the next Pope being a Muslim.

Activity 11
This activity will help you to improve your sales presentations.
A Analyse the last credentials presentation you made against the suggestions contained in this chapter. Any room for improvement?

Think about the last successful credentials presentation you made and analyse it. Why do you think it worked?

Think about the last unsuccessful credentials presentation you made (ie when you knew that there was a live project but you were not asked to go any further). What do you think went wrong?

B Dig a few of your past proposals out of the files. Can you find any room for improvement?

Take the suggested list of contents given in this chapter for a full competitive proposal, and see which of them can be held on a word processed template (or selection of templates), and which will need writing every time.

C Think carefully about the last three successful pitches you made. Why did they work? If you are not sure, ask your clients. Most will be pleased to tell you.

Then think about some unsuccessful pitches. Why did they fail? If you feel that you can, phone the contact concerned to ask why – distance from the event might help them to be frank with you.

D If you are against free pitching, write up your own list of arguments, based on those given in this chapter, that you believe will convince prospects, and which could form the basis for discussing the issue should anyone ask you to do it.

12 JUST HANG ON TO WHAT YOU'VE GOT: CLIENT CARE AND DEVELOPMENT

'Experience is the name everyone gives to their mistakes.'
Oscar Wilde: *Lady Windermere's Fan*

- From mountains to molehills
- New business? Old business?
- The client journey
- Client care
- Good and bad service
- Causes of dissatisfaction
- Management of dissatisfaction
- Client development: moving deeper
- Client development: moving wider
- Ten tips for client service
- And finally…

From mountains to molehills

If you allow client individuals to drift away, you will need to do more work at the cold approach end of your marketing programme. It therefore makes sense to encourage your clients to come back time and time again, and with larger and larger projects. Suggestions for marketing activities aimed at prospective clients have taken up most of this book. This chapter will deal with client care, client development and relationship marketing.

The effort needed to convert a prospect into an active client varies dramatically with the needs and the frame of mind of the person you are trying to persuade. It stands to reason, doesn't it? If someone has never heard of you and does not know what you are offering, they will be harder to convince than someone who has both heard of you and experienced your work. If they do not need design consultancy services at all, they will be impossible to convince. You cannot sell to someone who does not need – or know that they need – your services. In between, there are various shades of grey hillsides to climb. In the following chart, Level 6 is Everest, and Level 1 the molehill.

How do you get to the point when you are regularly kicking molehills flat rather than scaling treacherous mountains? By a concerted and systematic programme of client care and development.

Client Conversion	
Conversion difficulty level	*Indication of client's frame of mind*
6	I don't need design consultancy services
	I've never heard of your company
	I don't know what you can do for me
	Why are you bothering me?
5	I need design consultancy services
	I've never heard of your company
	I don't know what you can do for me
	Why should I give you any time?
4	I need design consultancy services
	I have heard of your company
	I don't know what you can do for me
	I might be prepared to listen
3	I need design consultancy services
	I have heard of your company
	I believe you might be able to do something for me
	Let's talk; I'm listening
2	I need design consultancy services
	I have worked with your company before
	I know exactly what you can do for me
	Would you like to join a competitive tender/pitch?
1	I need design consultancy services
	I have worked with your company before
	I know exactly what you can do for me
	Just prepare a cost estimate and time schedule; no competitors.

New business? Old business?

As well as new business development, there is old business development, and it is here that many design companies fail.

Sometimes we need to be reminded that our current client list comprises both companies and the individuals in them. Design companies tend to list client companies in their brochures and in credentials presentations – and it is the companies which other potential clients will be interested in. However, it is the individuals who are the most important to your future commercial success; they will decide whether or not to work with you again. It is also the individuals who will eventually move to a second company and who, if you have done your job properly, will introduce you to their new organization. Some design companies owe the majority of their current client company list to the influence of one peripatetic client individual.

Once you have become established, your business will come from two sources:

1 Existing client individuals coming back for more, either for the same company or organization or for a new one

2 New client individuals, some of whom might work for the same company or organization as one of your existing clients, and some of whom will be from new companies

Repeat business is the best indicator of a client's confidence in your abilities, and it starts projects off on a positive footing. It also reassures potential clients when your existing clients return for more; you are obviously doing a good job for them.

It is not possible to give a categorical rule about how much of your business should come from each source, but as a general guideline you should aim to get at least half from existing clients. Not only is the cost of retaining and developing a current client significantly lower than the cost of gaining a new one, but the potential profit level of work done for people and companies you know tends to be greater. For a start, you will be able to shorten the project learning curve. You will already know a great deal about the company, its brands and products and services, its way of operation, its market and its competitors and, since much design development is of necessity a case of trial and error, you will find that you waste less time and fewer resources in the pursuit of unsuitable solutions. You will already have a feel for what will and will not work, and as long as you do not allow your thinking to become stale or too channelled down a particular path, your clients will benefit from that knowledge.

The client journey

Within your programme, you will have individuals at four different stages of development.

1 Prospective clients

These are the people on your AA and KIT new business databases. Your aim is to convert them to the next stage.

2 Active or current clients

Those individuals for whom you have work in progress.

3 Dormant clients

The individuals for whom no work is currently going through the studio. Some will have very recently fallen asleep, and some of these will just be having a short nap before commissioning you to do the next project. Others, however, will be doing a good impersonation of Rip van Winkle, and the longer they have been asleep, the harder it is to wake them.

4 Ex-clients

Most non-active clients are, in fact, dormant. Few clients are genuinely ex, unless you have seriously failed them. If a client individual decides not to work with you any more they don't usually make a formal announcement of their intended departure. They simply drift away. They fail to reappoint you. Often, the first you hear of it is in the press, or when you see new work on the market which you could have done, but didn't.

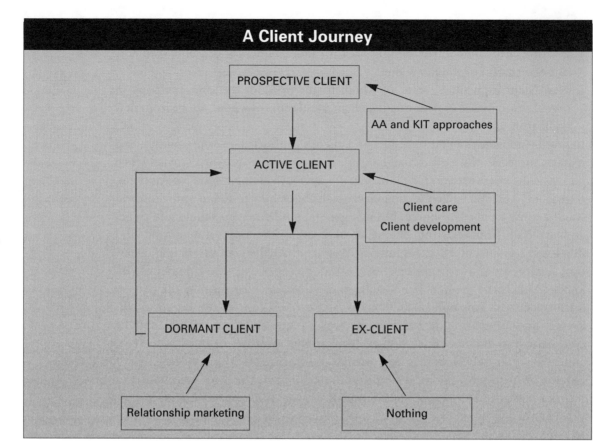

The activities you undertake and the results you achieve will determine at which stage on the journey a client is at any given moment (as in the chart below). For prospective client individuals, you will use a combination of bullseye and broadshot approaches – the AA and KIT methods described in Chapter 7. For active clients, you will use customer care and development activities. For dormant clients, a different sort of KIT method, that of relationship marketing, is needed. For genuine ex-clients, who are not going to consider using your services again, you can and need do nothing.

Client care

Excellence in quality and excellence in client care go hand in hand. There is a simple magic formula – one of the very few which work – for guaranteeing that you get repeat business, assuming that repeat business is there to be got. Some clients, of course, do not need design consultancy services very often.

The magic formula is:

Excellent work + excellent value for money + excellent service = repeat business

Picture it as a three-legged stool: you need all three legs if the stool is going to stand up. One or two are not enough. An added advantage to this analogy is that a three-legged stool is much more stable on rough ground than a stool or chair with any other number of legs.

Let's take a look at these three elements in detail:

1 Excellent work

- Is appropriate for its task. If creativity and high impact are required, it delivers. If something much more restrained or evolutionary is needed, it provides it. However, it can be useful to think of good work as being 'fit for the purpose, plus a bit'. It is often that extra touch – as long as it is appropriate – which makes the difference.

- Achieves the desired results. It works in its marketplace. We should all be striving to make sure that design work is as effective and as accountable as possible. This means that we need to help our clients to improve design briefs so that we set realistic objectives, and so that we understand how the results are going to be measured and evaluated.

- Is well received within the client's own organization. If it is hated by the commissioning client's boss and colleagues, it will not be too long before it is also hated by the client, no matter how appropriate or effective it has been.

2 Excellent value for money

- Is not the same as cheap. We all know excellent value for money when we experience it, even if the item in question costs a small fortune. One of the problems that design companies have when charging for their time is that a major project can seem inexpensive, while a tiny project can seem extortionate. We should be asking ourselves why we are selling time, like manual labourers, when we should be selling products and results.

- Is felt to be competitive within its own sector. No client would expect a top ten design consultancy to charge the same as a local freelancer – unless the top ten company has failed to point out why they charge considerably more.

3 Excellent service

- Meets intellectual needs, by responding quickly, accurately and with smooth progress. Challenges like being on or before time, on or under budget and perfectly on brief meet intellectual needs.

- Meets emotional needs, such as the provision of a good atmosphere for your clients to work in (yes, clients as well as employees). Emotional needs encompass the mood of your company, and the attitude of your staff towards its clients. This comes from the top: if senior management think that clients are a darned nuisance or a barrier to producing the best possible design, there is no hope for the rest of the company. You should be striving to make your clients actually want to work with you, and not with a more lively bunch of people down the road. There is little excuse for a design consultancy being dull, but it is surprising how many are.

Causes of dissatisfaction

Given that the formula for encouraging repeat business from happy clients is so simple, it is not very hard to turn that around to find the causes of dissatisfaction. Clients will be unhappy when they receive either poor work, or poor value for money, or poor service, or any combination of these, against their expectations.

Here, it is the expectations which are critical. If you promise a rose garden, and deliver a bunch of petunias, you only have yourself to blame if the disappointed client moves to new pastures next time they need design services. If you deliver a rose garden with an unexpected scented rose in it, you should have a happy client. Equally, if you promise petunias and deliver petunias, you will also have a happy client. The failure to meet expectations is the cause of the breakdown of all relationships, and the balance between disappointment and delight is very finely weighted indeed. Watch it like a hawk.

As a part of the management of expectations, try to develop a formal, written client care programme. It is wise to include all of your staff in its development so that they will feel fully committed to carrying it out and encouraged to use their initiative where appropriate.

Management of dissatisfaction

Praise is often silent, but criticism is usually stated. If you don't believe this, think how ready we all are to complain when something goes wrong in shops, or garages, or restaurants or with our own business suppliers, compared with how many times we actually take the trouble to thank or praise someone.

However, although criticism is usually stated, it is not always voiced to you. Studies carried out by The Tack Organisation, a human resource development specialist, clearly show that the clients to worry about are not those who tell you that they are unhappy with an aspect of your work, value for money or service – these are the helpful ones – but the ones who do not (see the chart below).

So who would a client tell of their dissatisfaction with you? Their boss, their juniors and their colleagues in their company, for a start. Their advisors in related businesses such as PR, advertising, marketing and management consultancy – the third parties. The media, in passing, if they were really unhappy. Their boss, juniors and colleagues in any new companies they move to. Their acquaintances at industry functions whenever the subject of design came up. Their friends and family members working in similar fields. Is that enough?

One simple remedy to this is a process which should be the last stage of any design project, carried out immediately before the final invoice is sent. This is a formal, post-project evaluation. Ideally, a senior member of your company, and preferably one who has not been closely involved in the project itself, should meet the commissioning client and work through an assessment of whether the client's own expectations of the work, of the value and of the service have been met. As a minimum, a post-completion questionnaire should be issued; many design companies offer to send a small donation to a specified charity (usually one of their clients, or related to their work) in return for each completed questionnaire.

Dissatisfied Customers

Dissatisfied customers who complain	4%
Dissatisfied customers who do not complain	96%
Dissatisfied customers who:	80%
• do not complain	
• but do not come back	
Dissatisfied customers who:	20%
• do not complain	
• do not come back	
• and tell more than ten others of their dissatisfaction	
Source: The Tack Organisation	

The important thing in either case is to have a structured process whereby the results can be compared with the results from other projects, and be tracked and measured over time. Apart from the fact that the information is vital to you if you are going to continue to improve your product, value and service, it will allow the client to express any concerns in a formal but constructive way, which will allow you to manage their expectations better the next time around. It quite simply makes the next time more likely.

A happy client is not only the best source of business from repeat commissions, but also an ambassador for your company. Turning your clients into advocates – even into missionaries – for your services is one of the best marketing investments you will ever make.

Client development: moving deeper

A good client care and development programme will bring you not only repeat business, but better business. This includes larger, more stimulating and/or more profitable projects commissioned by clients as their confidence in you grows. This is what is known as moving deeper into a client's organization.

In part, this sort of development happens naturally as you work more intensively with a client; gradually, they will become aware of other skills and abilities that you possess, and will have learnt that you can be trusted to produce the right work, at the right price, with the right level of service.

However, it is very easy to become pigeon-holed in the client's perception into being a specialist provider of one type of service, and we need to take active measures to counteract this tendency. This is where the process of relationship marketing helps. This comprises two elements: qualitative and quantitative.

Qualitatively, it is important that you remember to talk to your clients about the work you have completed for other companies, and which is in the public domain. Obviously, you must never discuss or show any confidential work in progress. Secondly, having examples of your work in the reception area or in meeting rooms also helps clients to form an overall view of your capabilities.

Quantitatively, it means creating a separate KIT database for your current and dormant clients, and mailing them exactly the sorts of things which you are mailing to prospects, but with a much more pertinent letter. A campaign like this needs every bit as much thought and management as those you prepare for prospective clients. As a further part of the KIT process, it is helpful to send them press cuttings of items of interest, or to phone them whenever a suitable reason presents itself. The idea is to keep you and your company at the top of their mind.

Your objective will be to increase the number and the value of the commissions from a given customer individual. Your method will be to establish the budgets in the control of that individual, identify which competitive companies, or internal departments, are getting that budget, and develop a plan for asking for the business.

Client development: moving wider

Here, your objective is to gain commissions from other individuals in a current client's department, division, or sister company, in your own country or abroad. It works on the principle that if you approach people to whom you have been given an introduction by your current client, they will be more inclined to spare you some time. It also indicates that you are – whether in a formal sense or not – already an approved supplier to their own company.

Your method is not dissimilar to that needed for moving more deeply into a client's organization, but it will be more complex since more than one entry point will need to be identified. First, you will need to draw up the structure of the department or division or company, including the individuals and their jobs or roles. This will start to give you the reporting structure. The next stage is to identify the design work being commissioned by these people, and which competitive companies, or internal departments, are getting the budgets. Lastly, you need to develop an action plan for asking for an introduction to the people you want to talk to. Never go behind your current client's back; not only is it wise to enlist their help, but you will run the risk of making an enemy if you approach their colleagues without their knowledge.

Ten tips for client service

1 Manage each client individual's expectations:
   - find out what they expect
   - communicate exactly what you can (and can't) deliver
   - never over-promise
   - never under-deliver.
2 Make sure that all of your design recommendations are on brief:
   - any other recommendations made should be in addition to, not instead of, those which are expected.
3 Deliver work on or before time, and on or under budget. Set up a full alert system to go into operation if either is impossible:
   - by phone
   - by fax
   - by follow-up letter with a revised estimate.
4 Specify everything in writing, in advance:
   - design strategy and creative brief
   - production specifications
   - terms of business/contracts
   - cost estimates
   - timing schedules.
5 Demonstrate attention to detail in all of your recommendations, project management and implementation. If necessary, set up improved systems for quality control.
6 Keep clients informed at all stages of their project:
   - have regular work sessions with your clients
   - telephone frequently with progress reports
   - supply written summaries of all meetings and telephone conversations where action is agreed, whether or not the client was present (for example with suppliers).

7 Know your client:
- company, product, brand or service needs
- business operations and environment
- competitors
- views, opinions, beliefs, feelings, knowledge.

8 Make sure all of the members of your own company know:
- who the clients are
- a little about their business
- the work you are doing for them.

9 Make sure clients are greeted by name, and warmly, as honoured guests:
- at reception
- on the telephone.

10 Make sure that your clients are informed about, understand and feel comfortable with all aspects of your company:
- give them staff names to contact
- make sure they are familiar with your building(s)
- explain your working systems
- show them non-confidential work for other clients
- make them feel at home.

And finally...

There is an old and admirable belief that the business of being in business is to make a profit and have fun. If you don't make a profit, you will not be in business for very much longer. If you don't enjoy working in your chosen business area, you should make a change; people who are fortunate enough to be in employment spend too many waking hours at work to be miserable doing it.

If you find that you are getting neither profit nor fun by working with a client, and if the situation cannot be remedied by discussion and negotiation, do not hesitate to say your farewells. If, on the other hand, you are able to work with clients who allow you to make a profit and produce satisfying work, go that little bit further – the extra mile – for them. Make the effort. Provide a real service, with a genuine smile.

It can take four years or more of hard work and a large investment in both time and funds to gain a client. Losing them happens very much faster, often without your even noticing. It is not enough to simply meet your clients' needs – you should be anticipating them. It is not enough to meet their expectations – you need to exceed them. In his *Discourse on Method*, the French philosopher René Descartes said: 'It is not enough to have a good mind; the main thing is to use it properly.' Make sure that every single person in your company uses their 'client-facing' mind to the best effect. Keep caring, keep developing: keep your clients.

Activity 12

This final activity will start you thinking in a structured way about the care and development of your current clients

A Thinking of one of your client individuals:
- develop a plan for moving more deeply into his or her company culture, so that you win more business from that individual
- now develop a plan for moving more widely through that individual's organization.

B Repeat the exercise for each of your key client individuals in turn. You will soon begin to see some potential areas for development.

C With your colleagues, develop a formal client care/client service charter, perhaps using some of the tips from this chapter. If you can, involve all of your staff in its creation, in order to get full commitment. Finally, don't forget to show it to your clients.

PART II

The Practice: How it is done

THE PRACTICE: HOW IT IS DONE

'The Golden Rule is that there are no Golden Rules.'
George Bernard Shaw, *Man and Superman*

This section contains contributions from leading European design practitioners who have been generous in sharing some of the secrets of their considerable commercial achievements. The wide diversity of their marketing beliefs and behaviour clearly demonstrates that there are more ways than one of putting the principles into practice.

However, even though their marketing strategies and plans are very varied, the continuing success of these top professionals indicates two important things:

- They all have an excellent design product, which clients want to buy again and again. This is backed up in turn by matching levels of service; you will hear most of them talk about their conscious efforts to remain client-focused at all times.
- Each of them has a very clear idea of their company's positioning in the marketplace, who their target markets are, what offers they are able to make to those target markets, and how to reach them. In other words, they are building firmly on the four cornerstones of strategic marketing.

The individuals who have contributed to this section were either interviewed in person and by telephone or were participants in a DBA (Design Business Association) debate on the subject. There is a full list on pages viii–ix.

The text is simply a lightly edited version of the interview or speech as recorded, and is intended to capture all of the spontaneity and vigour of the individuals concerned. In each case, the text has been approved for publication. However, it is important to note that although the views given were current at the time, it is quite possible that, as time elapses, the marketing programmes of the company concerned might have taken an entirely new direction, or that the individual might have moved to another company. In marketing, as in design, nothing remains static for long.

20/20, LONDON, UK
Richard Mott

- Our natural enthusiasm for our business and for our clients' business, plus training in presentation and communication, enables us to put across our story well. Our approach is very clear and very well thought through, so it almost sells itself.

At 20/20, we have identified and developed a unique business; we combine retail strategy, store design and interactive technology, and we focus on major change. We've done this through a careful study of our marketplace – retail – and an awareness of our strengths, which are our experience, our innovation, our passion and our total focus on customers.

All of our UK work comes to us. We have now established ourselves sufficiently to be included on many retailers' shortlists. Sometimes the list is drawn up by the client, and sometimes by EDR (European Design Register). Once we are shortlisted and have the opportunity to meet a client, we will usually win the project, if it is a client who is right for us – we do not suit all clients. It is, of course, much harder to establish a high profile abroad. Sometimes our profile in the UK is sufficiently high to be seen from afar; otherwise we invest time in getting to know the major players in selected target countries where we believe our approach will fit well.

All 20/20's directors and top management are responsible for business development as a part of their role. PR is very important to us, and one person in-house plans and drives PR activity. My partner Bernard Dooling acts as our mouthpiece to the press – he is great at delivering quotable material. We will also speak at conferences, write articles and so on.

We always record our major projects, and spend a lot of time and effort doing so. We produce separate brochures for each one, which we mainly use to follow up face-to-face sessions rather than as mailshots. Good photography is the key. A picture is worth a thousand words, and a great picture gets you seen and remembered.

CARRE NOIR, PARIS, FRANCE
Gérard Caron

- At the moment, a lot of design consultancies feel that they have to say: 'Yes, yes, yes' to everything the client suggests. But for the client, it is very important to have a real design partner who can say: 'No, I don't agree with you; we will have to think a little bit more about that.'

Carré Noir was the first design agency in France to offer not only a design service but also a marketing service. In 1973 that was quite new, and we gained a unique position in the market by putting marketing and design people under one roof. From the beginning, we decided to offer all of the design services needed by a company: this means the identification of the company; of its products through packaging and, to a small extent, industrial design; of its point of purchase through retail signage and interior design; and of its permanent communication system through its corporate literature and multimedia. Now we have 120 people worldwide, with offices in Paris, London, Brussels, Turin and Tokyo, and we also have a partnership with a marketing company in New York.

Our marketing approach may be different from our competitors, certainly in France, because we don't prospect (cold call), or at least very little. The fame Carré Noir has means that between 90 and 95 per cent of our clients come by themselves – they ring us. We are very lucky in that way, but of course it is not by accident. From the beginning, our policy was just to keep to the same road: to bring quality to strategies and methodology, both in design and marketing. It is a very high level policy. Since 1973 we have designed 9 000 products, 1 000 corporate identities and 90 concepts for interior point of sale, and that is how we have built our reputation. People know that our lowest level is good, and that our normal level is very good. This forms our advertising and promotional campaign.

We also have a good relationship with the media, and I am personally very involved with our PR activities. I speak at conferences, give lectures, meet students, do TV and radio shows and so on. We have a full-time PR office of two people within our company, and they give global direction to our local companies, who continue the work in their own countries.

Over 60 per cent of our clients have been with us for more than four years. We produce good work, of course, but that is not enough by itself; we also have a close relationship with our clients. Carré Noir may be a big company, but we work alongside our clients in very small teams – three or four people, no more. Our clients know these people well. They keep control of the job from beginning to end and so it is easy for them to maintain a good relationship. People know each other; I would not like to have a pyramid organization where our President has to meet their President and so on.

Unlike some design agencies, we do not feel that we have to always agree with our clients' briefs, even if the market is more competitive than before. Obviously, it's a big problem if you lose a client, and some clients try to put pressure on their design agencies; they will not accept any opposition. It's a pity. This kind of dialogue can be difficult at the moment with the recession, but it is very important. We must be a real partner to our clients.

THE CHASE, MANCHESTER, UK
Jan Wood

- Very often we would visit our own clients, and would see a huge pile of brochures from other design groups by their desks. We would think: 'Do they ever read them? Do any of them stand out?'

One of the problems we had when we started in 1986 was that although the two founding directors, Ben Casey and Lionel Hatch, had a lot of experience from working with other companies, they had nothing they could show for The Chase. They needed to get in to see clients, to get appointments, so they came up with a novel mailer – a box with a little carved sandalwood elephant in it. On the lid of the box was the story of an old Indian craftsman who, when asked how he managed to carve such beautiful sculptures, replied that he just cut away the bits of wood that didn't look like an elephant. We related this to our work: whenever client companies come to us, we need to decide not just what they are, but also what they are not. The mailer was very successful for us, because it gave people something to remember The Chase by, and gave an impression of the spirit and the philosophy of our company. It was a nice way of getting our message across, and the people who received it remembered it and were interested in talking to us. It proved very useful in the early days.

We didn't have a brochure for some time which, when you think that our work is 70 per cent corporate literature, is a bit like the decorator who never decorates his own house. We decided a couple of years ago to do something, but we didn't want to do another ordinary brochure that would end up in someone's filing cabinet or bin. We decided instead to publish a hardback book called *The Chase by The Chase*. We took a different tack from most design consultancies: we do not talk about how we can put X per cent on a client's business, or any other standard marketing promises. The book is about how we go about our work, where we get our ideas from, so that clients can get a better understanding of what happens. I think that there is still a mystique about design, about what happens between the brief and the presentation of the work. We used examples of our designs done over seven or eight years to illustrate the points. Again, the book has been very successful for us, because it is so different from what other design companies are doing.

A lot of the other marketing techniques we use are not really anything new; they are probably just the same as the ones everyone else is using. We don't do a lot of PR, and so we don't have someone constantly trying to create stories for us. There have been articles about us in the press, but they have come to us; perhaps we should be more pro-active about contacting them. We do, however, put a lot of emphasis on winning awards, and that always gets written about. We feel that if we concentrate on winning the awards, the PR will follow naturally.

COLEY PORTER BELL, LONDON, UK
Colin Porter

● Information is free; in design, we do not use it enough.

The company was formed as a breakaway from Fitch, so we were fortunate that some of our clients decided to come with us. Right from the start, we had no difficulty getting clients, for example Guinness and Marks & Spencer. They sustained us for five or six years, and thank God we had them – we were just coming out of a recession, which was ironically a good time to start a company. In the early 1980s, packaging enjoyed a focus as never before. Advertising and marketing expenditure was being looked at, and there was a retail revolution going on with, for example, Sainsbury looking seriously at its products and the quality of its offer. It seemed that many FMCG companies were discovering marketing for the first time, and designers were convincing people that marketing and design went together. We were fortunate to follow Michael Peters, Fitch and Wolff Olins.

At first there were only three people in Coley Porter Bell. All we did in the way of marketing was to write letters, do credentials presentations and refuse to speak to journalists (we were scared of them). Our success rate was about one in 200, and there was a lot of stress and a lot of rejections. But it was like a drug – the wins kept us going. Our pattern became one of: go out, get work, do work, realize no more work, go out etc. Believe me, that is no way to run a business! You've got to put the effort into marketing and do it 100 per cent of the time, which is what Coley Porter Bell does now. We saw the last recession coming, and did not rush to look overseas. We saw more potential in the UK market, and followed our UK clients in their own European expansion.

We divide marketing into two activities: hunting (the cold calling) and farming (development of current business). We have two teams responsible for new business and client servicing, reporting directly to the management team. The account managers are responsible for maintaining relationships with existing clients and ensuring all opportunities are followed up; there are currently two heads of account management who are both on the board. This farming is coordinated by the new business department at monthly meetings. As part of the farming process, we run workshops for clients, for example Cadbury and Van den Bergh, whose young recruits know nothing about design. These workshops are paid for by the clients.

Hunting is generally dealt with by the new business team. We have dedicated telesales people who also maintain the database, as well as a marketing manager and a new business director. The whole process is summarized on a weekly new business report which is circulated to all key personnel.

We are constantly looking for opportunities to raise our profile via PR, and we have a freelance consultant who works two days a week for us. She targets conference speaking opportunities, writes press articles, comes up with ideas for research projects and generally ensures that our reputation is sustained externally.

Coley Porter Bell is part of the WPP Group, and we did not at first make the most of it in terms of networks. However, we are doing so now, for example with the advertising agencies JWT and O&M. Our activities are also directed to selling within the largest organizations.

We always conduct client surveys, for example asking why Coley Porter Bell won (or lost) a pitch, and we send out regular client satisfaction surveys. We try to be consistent with our marketing message.

DESIGN BOARD, BRUSSELS, BELGIUM
Martin van Grevenstein

- A salesman is only as good as the company he is selling. I don't believe that marketing techniques will do the trick; it is foremost a question of getting your product right.

When you are marketing a design company, I personally believe that the first thing you have to do is to clarify your positioning. You need to know what you want to communicate and what your product is, what your strengths and weaknesses are, and where you want to go. Secondly, you need to take into account your company's specific situation, track record and history. I don't believe that there is one Golden Rule of a marketing strategy for every design company. The third thing is that you have to have six or seven different tools to communicate and market yourself, and each tool has a different purpose. In general, I would say use them all, whenever they are appropriate, but recognize that they are different.

Design Board was founded in 1983 and we have our European design centre in Brussels, employing six or seven nationalities. We also have an office in Paris, called Aesthete, which specializes in perfume and luxury goods design, a company in Madrid called Communicarte/Design Board, and we have a link with a US company called LAGA. Ninety per cent of our work is international, developing and managing brand packaging. Our clients are based right across Europe; Brussels does not have a big domestic market, unlike London or Paris, so we have to look for clients worldwide. The methods we use are similar for all countries, but it means that we have to be quite selective about whom we contact. We can't go to every company, so we focus quite strongly.

Our list of marketing priorities starts with our clients – clients, clients, clients. We do the best possible work for them and try to earn their loyalty and grow the account. Our first source of business is referrals. The second marketing area for us is what I would call image communications: PR, brochures, attending seminars and so on. It's about telling people who we are in the way we want to tell it. Thirdly we have a large database, and there's quite a bit of cold calling and mailings as a standard procedure. Design Board has been on the market for quite a time now, and our situation is not like that of a new company when you would have to get people to notice you; it's much more a matter of maintaining contacts and relationships. There's always a certain amount of cold calling to do, but it is third on the list. And fourthly we occasionally have very specific marketing activities, such as organizing a seminar for clients or doing a study on a certain subject and presenting it to potential clients. That's about the sum of it. We do not have full-time marketing people – our account directors are responsible for new business as well as current business. We use external resources for PR, organizing seminars and sometimes for telemarketing.

I have worked with several design companies and seen all sorts of methods used, and I know that there is not just one way of doing it. I do know, however, that there are some ways of not doing it – you can't just use sales techniques. In the end, the thing that makes the difference is how good you are, and how clear you are about what you can offer.

DESIGN BRIDGE, LONDON, UK
David Rivett

- The one constant in business is change. If you treat it as an enemy, it will get you. If you befriend it, you can use it as a springboard, because you might anticipate something before anyone else does. Accommodating and using change is fundamental to success.

My view on marketing anything, not just design, is very pragmatic. It's about using common sense. It's always enormously powerful, and clients respond well to it. A lot of consultancies make the mistake of saying to potential clients: 'You may think you've got a simple problem, but actually it's much more complicated than that.' I see our job as the very reverse of that: it's to make simplicity out of complexity. Design Bridge has always recognized that the commercial objectives of our clients are important. They basically want a bottom-line result. It happens to be design that they are talking to us about, but they are also talking to their distribution channels and to their computer systems people about ways of getting that same result. The bridge between commercial reality and outstanding design is fundamental to our business, and we tend to have as many marketeers as designers.

The ideal marketing situation for any consultancy is not to have to sell. It is to build a solid base of clients by recommendation, by word of mouth. The best management consultants in the world very rarely sell overtly, and I think that we should aspire to the same degree of recognition and recommendation. We'd like to be top-of-mind at the top of our clients' organizations, which means working our way up the value chain so that we deal with progressively more senior people.

We have tried to add more value around our core design service. That has taken different forms: the introduction of Design Bridge Structure, for example, wrapped an enormous amount of additional value around our graphics offer and took us into the area of three-dimensional branding. Looking to the future, we want to add other offers which are complementary to our client base and our core activities, such as proprietary market research and new product development (NPD) methodologies. All the time we are addressing our product and adding value to it, so that the combination of services starts to build an offer which is different from those of our competitors. It's the combination that's important: you take common ingredients and put them together in an unconventional way.

When Design Bridge started, we had a couple of good relationships with clients, and we nurtured and cherished those relationships for all they were worth. It's what you've got to do when you start. Those relationships will have an almost biological habit of subdividing and multiplying. People will leave your core clients and go to another company, so suddenly you have a foothold in another business, and then yet another. You've still kept the core clients, you hope, but the word has progressively spread. In that way, by starting with two or three really solid clients, by building very strong personal contacts with people in those companies, by servicing them to death, and by really becoming part of their team, you can form relationships which will pass beyond their mother companies and on to other companies across the world.

We have a full service office in Amsterdam, a joint venture in India with Lintas, and an agent and office in Indonesia. We market ourselves internationally in the same way as to the domestic market. It was built into the business on Day One that this is an international company. We think internationally, we look at international brands. We find it difficult to see a distinction between something that we are doing in Manchester or Milan. One of our strengths – and it is important when you are selling internationally – is our awareness of different cultural norms in different parts of the world.

We do very little cold calling – almost none. We do identify target sectors where we feel we haven't got as much exposure as we would like, and we will then take some sort of initiative. It is pointless to just go in and say; 'We are the XYZ Design company, and we would love to work with you.' You have to deliver something of value in your first conversation. For example, it might be an insight into the potential client's communication mix or their product format. The approach might bear no fruit for some while, but at least the seeds have been sown, and that's what you've got to be prepared to do in terms of cultivating new business.

PR is very important to us. I have a huge amount of sympathy with PR people because it's their job to communicate what we have to say, not to think what we should be saying in the first place. I think a lot of people approach PR in the wrong way, and expect their PR company to be thinking their thoughts for them, and then it doesn't work.

One basic principle we follow at Design Bridge is never to be afraid of investing in the best people, either internally or externally. Good people always deliver much more than their cost. Always invest in the best.

Overall, a narrow marketing focus will always be more productive than a broad focus. You need to look at where you can be better than your competitors. It may only be by a margin, it may be simply that your chemistry is better, but you need to identify something, however narrowly defined, which lets you really stand out, and just build on that. It may look a terribly small foundation, but build on it.

We are in the fortunate position of having enquiries coming over the transom. If we convert enough of those, we don't have to go seeking for clients, other than those from specific sectors or companies which we would love to work with. But it is terribly important to have a pro-active response to anything that moves. There's a hierarchy of new business. The client you've got is always going to be the most cost-effective to get new business from, if you deliver a tremendously high service. The next will be the potential client who contacts you, so you have to make sure that you respond absolutely 150 per cent to them. The most expensive will be the person who's never heard of you, and doesn't know what you sell.

DIN ASSOCIATES, LONDON, UK
Rasshied Din

- A lot of our new business effort is really down to answering the phone.

The company was founded in 1986. How did we get work from clients? For three years, I could not have told you. Things just happened; the phone kept ringing. In 1989, we did a DTI Marketing Initiative programme. The recommendations made were to upgrade our literature every six months, get run-ons of articles about us, set up a database, set up a mailshot programme, establish monthly targets, write new business letters and create two or three different portfolios. But we were too busy to do any of that at the time, so we didn't do it.

Our business develops on recommendations and word of mouth; this happens because of the way we work. We create press coverage and publicity about our work, and spend a fortune on photography – the best we can afford. Leads to the press often come through the photographers. We also put work in for competitions: if it wins or is shortlisted, people see it. The best PR we have comes from our clients, as word of mouth. When we opened a store on New Bond Street, we had 14 enquiries in a week. Foreign work has also been gained by word of mouth or by people having seen our work on the high street although it is really important to sort out the contract details beforehand with foreign work. There is also a danger of spreading yourself too thinly, and therefore affecting other current clients.

The main issue for us is how we keep our clients, not how we find them. We offer a personal service, direct contact with the designers and a quick response. We encourage a high level of client involvement, and we set realistic goals on their behalf. We also motivate our staff – they are the representatives of our business. We give them challenging work and remunerate them well.

I'm not convinced about letter writing. Over two years, I wrote more than 70 letters and had ten replies, one interview and no work.

The way we sell is that we don't sell. We have a non-sales approach. We try to build long-term relationships with our clients.

ELMWOOD, LEEDS, UK
Jonathan Sands

- One of our biggest successes is the fact that once we've got a client, we very rarely lose them. We spend most of our effort, even today, marketing ourselves to our existing clients rather than to new ones. If we are helping them grow, then they are helping us to grow.

The real thing, in fact the only thing, that has developed Elmwood's business is the quality of our product. Without a good product, all the marketing in the world will have little long-term effect. And by the product, I don't just mean the creative product: I mean everything – the service, the price, our approach, everything! Having said this, of course we do try and spread the word through marketing.

At first, our marketing was very haphazard, often just knee-jerk reaction stuff. Someone may phone from a directory or a creative magazine with a special deal, and we'd take it. When times got a bit quiet we would put our heads together and come up with a direct mailshot. We also started to enter, and win, design awards. However, our single most successful new business tactic in the beginning was telephone sales. Virtually all of our business came through us getting on the telephone, asking to see people and presenting a portfolio. Our success rate was very high; we knew that once we'd got in front of potential clients, we could convert a good proportion of them. For every 20 telephone calls, we'd get to see one or two companies, and we would convert one in three meetings into a piece of business. We were very telesales driven and sold on our personalities – potential clients either really loved our style or found absolutely no empathy with us at all. This black-and-white reaction is still very true today.

Things changed with the recession. Competition was much fiercer, and clients hadn't got time to see companies like us. In addition, our telesales became far less successful with the advent of voicemail and secretaries getting better at fending off our calls. By the early 1990s, when we had started to develop other design disciplines such as corporate identity and annual reports as well as our original strength, packaging design, we knew that we had to be more structured in our marketing approach. We needed a proper plan, and we started to budget for an annual marketing spend. We had specific direct mailshots: one for report and accounts, one for packaging, and so on. We advertised in a number of directories. We put great emphasis on our Christmas cards, for which we started to gain a reputation. We also organized a lot of events, such as days at the races, golfing days, and go-karting days.

This straightforward marketing activity worked reasonably well, and we grew, but it was still ad hoc. There wasn't a strong corporate style to our own promotional work, as we designed everything as an individual tactical piece.

Nevertheless, by 1993, Elmwood had established itself in the marketplace. I had become a Director of the DBA, which was a testimony to the fact that people saw Elmwood as a credible force, and we'd won a couple of Clios and a number of major design awards. We were definitely doing something right, but I suspect that it was more to do with our personality and the goodwill we had with our existing clients than any fantastic marketing we were doing.

The end of 1993 was a key time for us. We realized that we were in the first division, playing in the top league with the likes of Coley Porter Bell, Lewis Moberly and Design Bridge. But what made Elmwood different? Why did people choose us rather than somebody else? If we didn't know what our point of difference was, how could we market ourselves properly to our potential clients?

We took all of our key members of staff away for two days, and got six outside consultants, one of them a respected competitor, to give us a real going-over. We showed them our client list, our marketing plans and our financial performance and said: 'Right, this is who we are and where we are; let's sort out where we want to be and how we are going to get there.' As a result of that two-day brainstorming session, we came up with six individual strategic plans covering six different aspects of our business.

Today, we have a really different proposition for Elmwood, and this is manifested in our book. It's not a standard design consultancy brochure; it has a cover price and is sold in shops. It is about our beliefs and the way we do things, and it's based on two things. Success has to be externally, or client, driven because in order to grow you have to satisfy clients' needs. But to grow successfully you also have to grow from within. You have to enjoy what you do; if you enjoy something, you're going to get better at it. We have therefore created an internal vision of how we want to be, which is that design is at the centre of everything we do – we should be a living manifestation of the design process. We also have an external vision, which has been influenced by all sorts of people, including Tom Peters' book *The Pursuit of Wow*, and Harvard Business School people like Gary Hamel and his book *Competing for the Future*.

We paraphrase our point of difference like this. All businesses are in a race that none of them will ever win. There can be no winners because there is no finish line – just a dynamic arena in which conditions are always changing: the marketplace, the economic climate, the spirit of the times, the other competitors. The challenge is to make the running, to force the pace. How do you do it? There are no easy answers. But successful companies all over the world have discovered that there is one vital key to success – design. Not pretty design, not safe design – but design that understands the nature of the race. At Elmwood, we have to deliver benefits to clients which will enable them to lead that race. It might not be design solutions; it could be all sorts of benefits. We want clients to use us to do something new, and so we believe that every time we do a project we should rewrite the rules. We think laterally about our clients and their brands, so that we come up with innovative solutions.

Having found ourselves and developed these wonderful strategic plans doesn't mean to say that we throw all our old marketing techniques out of the window.

Some of them must still be right; after all, they have helped us to get where we are now and are part of our personality. We are still going to do some of the tactical things that we have always done. For example, we take part in the Marketing Forum on the *Canberra*; it has been quite successful for us. We will still do the Christmas card. But we now also have this positioning book which says why we are different. We call it a 'comfort factor document'. We are competing against the biggest design companies, most if not all of whom are based in London, and we are this enigma based in Leeds which has come from nowhere. This book – a visible, tangible thing – will show clients that we are a terrific design company; we hope it will help Elmwood leapfrog the competition. Not everybody will like our point of difference, but we take the view that those who like us will absolutely love us, while those who don't like us will probably hate us. However, as long as we have clients who stay ten years because they adore us, then that's the way we will go.

We also have an association with other European design companies through our network called Totem, and that is going from strength to strength. We don't use it specifically as a new business tool, but as a research resource for clients who want to export to Europe; they also act as a vetting agent. Once we've done the design work, they help us to assess whether it works in their market, for example whether it is legally correct or culturally appropriate. We also enjoy job swapping; by sending designers to each other, we learn how we market ourselves and how we work internally as well as externally. In virtually every country it's different.

We pay a lot of attention to our profile. We do seminars and we appear in the press so that, by putting ourselves in the right forum, it helps endorse the fact that we are experts in our subject. We also mix within industry events; it is as important to be respected by your peers as by your potential clients. We get lots of ideas on marketing and best practice from talking to our friendly competitors. We've spent time studying the marketplace, learning from other companies, and then doing it our way. Our success comes from planning our work, from being consistent in our approach, and from really understanding what our point of difference is, and therefore what our message should be.

IDEO PRODUCT DEVELOPMENT, LONDON, UK

Ingelise Nielsen

- We have a brochure in a large square format which sticks out on your shelf – you just have to pick it up. It doesn't fit in your bin either, so you have got to keep it.

In IDEO we been marketing ourselves pro-actively for some years. I've been working on it for about six years now, but the job has changed considerably with the growth of the company. I find that with the size we are now – we have over 200 people worldwide and just over 30 in London – cold calling has nearly disappeared. The effort is just too great for the payback, and we are very likely to get the clients who are not going to benefit the most from us and, vice versa, who might not benefit us. Over the years, the cold calling has been done but we are much more selective now. I think you just learn what kind of companies are likely to be well matched with you. I still research companies and try to get to know them, but the list is now very much smaller – maybe it's 30, 40, 50 top companies that I keep in close contact with. The days of sending out 200 mailshots went a long time ago.

Between 50 and 75 per cent of IDEO's work in London is repeat work, which means that we put a lot of effort into client management and client liaison. We want to exceed our clients' expectations all the time. I know that's a cliché statement at the moment, but it is true all the same. It's low cost; you get a lot of enjoyment out of it; the clients get much more benefit from it; and the payback is invaluable because they are likely to come back for more work. And it's not just the repeat work that's important. What often happens is that you are able to suggest things that your client ought to be working on, which means that you get the choice of work that you prefer to do as well. There is no set way of looking after our clients, just a generic set of rules. It varies with each one. All of our people are very involved, but then that's because we are a very flat organization. Everybody's pretty senior, and we all have our own client relationships.

Right at the beginning of a project, our clients know that we are making a conscious effort to look after them. They know, for example, that there's always someone who is not on the project that they can talk to. Say they are working with someone who is a brilliant designer and a good project leader, but there is a personality clash – it can happen. It is possible to lose that project or that client because nobody likes to say 'I don't like his or her manner.' If you have someone else in the office they can talk to, or someone who rings them up to ask how things are going and just keeps in touch in an informal way, it gives them the opportunity to say 'Well, it's fine but to be absolutely honest I just wish I was working with a different person.'

We have just started using an external PR company. It's something we haven't really done much in the past. We have relied on winning awards – which we've done incredibly well at – and on journalists coming to seek us out. We are now more pro-active in PR because we would like to get more of a presence in Europe.

Overall, I think the most important thing is to exceed your clients' expectations. You can be a very clever designer, but there are a lot of other clever designers out there. It's very hard for people setting up to be truly differentiated from the competition, but the way everybody can differentiate themselves is to do everything much, much better.

IMAGINATION, LONDON, UK
Ralph Ardill

- Our whole ethos for marketing Imagination is to create challenging and exciting experiences of the Imagination brand. To treat ourselves like our own clients.

For us, the two most important things are to know who our clients are, and to know what our offer is. We have a building full of architects, interior, graphic, multimedia, theatre, lighting and acoustic designers – the whole creative toolbox – along with the full logistical, technical and project management resource to bring our ideas to life. The biggest danger in having this kind of resource is to think that because we can potentially tackle almost any project, then everyone must be a potential client. A big mistake. Traditional marketing techniques such as segmenting audiences and looking at different geographical markets simply cannot work for us. We would find ourselves trying to get on the pitch list for every lighting project, every conference, every brochure. We would need a database the size of NASA's and a team of 50 people to run it! The big shift in our emphasis over the last couple of years has been the recognition that our future lies in the development of longer-term strategic relationships with a handful of key client companies, and probably with a small number of visionary individuals within those companies.

Given the diversity of our resource and capability, we had to find a way of articulating very quickly what we stand for, because a potential client could easily come here, walk around, experience this machine in action, and then walk out again thinking: 'I feel I should be talking to these people, but I don't know how to work with them, I don't know what they are offering me. They are exciting, but I don't quite know what they're going to do for me.'

To simplify matters, it is vital that our clients appreciate we are an ideas factory, not a media production line. We have no vested interest in any one 'off-the-shelf' media solution to our client's business and communication challenges. We simply exist to harness the unique power of our diverse creative resource to deliver the most appropriate, innovative and effective Brand Experience for any particular brief.

Having developed this Brand Experience positioning, we approach business development by looking at people as much as at companies. The clients we ultimately want to work with invariably possess three values. They will have the vision to appreciate the totality and relevance of our Brand Experience offer, they will have the political power to motivate their organizations into supporting and taking ownership of this vision, and they will have the budget, however large or small, to make this vision a reality.

It is not difficult to identify these people. They tend to be the ones you read about in the newspapers all the time. They are the movers, the shakers, the people who are demanding innovation, who are saying there must be life beyond advertising. They have often reached the top levels in their own organizations by having a philosophy not dissimilar to our own.

We have inroads into most client companies through a variety of means. One of our greatest assets is our building. A lot of people use it for functions; quite often, the chief executive and marketing director of a major international company will have just walked into the best consultancy they've never heard of. At Christmas, we have a tradition of decorating the front of the Imagination building with a huge display of festive lights. Again, a powerful and unique experience of the Imagination brand.

Sometimes I might simply write to a prospective client, but what I am able to say in a such a letter helps to set it apart from the letters they receive from other agencies. I am not trying to sell them a media product. I say: 'Look, there is a company here who is thinking about marketing and creativity the same way as you. And we are not only thinking about it, we are doing it, and we would like to talk to you about how we might work together.' It's a compelling statement, because the most cynical reaction I am going to get is: 'OK – prove it.' That's the only reaction that we need.

The strength of the Imagination brand itself brings in enquiries from all over the world. There is no shortage of projects coming in through the door, and the key new business challenge is often one of filtering and project selection as opposed to speculative cold calling. I am careful to make sure that the work we bring in is creatively rewarding, in line with our profit remit, and validates our core Brand Experience proposition.

To help us define and take ownership of the Brand Experience concept, we have put together a book on the subject. We spent a year researching the finest and most aspirational projects we could find around the world and across all media disciplines for a volume simply entitled *Experience*. Only three per cent of the work in it is ours: we simply wanted to encapsulate an attitude and a mode of thought. As it says in the book, its purpose is to 'inspire and challenge convention through an insight into some of the world's most innovative communication experiences'. We have since followed this publication with the launch of our own new corporate book called *Imagination*. This was developed to replace all of our previous marketing and corporate literature. It sets out the argument and philosophy behind our Brand Experience offer, which is then supported and validated by 20 years of Imagination project case histories, photography and ideas development.

We used to have all of the conventional tools of the trade, the corporate brochures, the profile documents, the credentials presentations and all the rest of it. We've done away with all of that. If I've got an hour with somebody, I'd rather spend the time talking about what we can do for them rather than what we have done for other people. We are also approaching clients now not with fee proposals, but with business plans for creative concepts and Brand Experience programmes.

We talk to them about how they might fund a project or programme, what the sponsorship opportunities are, what the media value is, what the on-going licensing and merchandizing opportunities are. We are working on more complicated but much more creatively rewarding projects, as part of establishing long-term strategic relationships with our clients.

It would be wonderful if in ten years' time Imagination was perceived from a design perspective as a college, and from a business point of view almost like a club, where if someone regards themselves as an entrepreneurial brand marketeer, they really ought to join. When you get to that point, your marketing almost takes care of itself.

There's no big 20-year plan for Imagination, and there can't be. We have to be in a position to respond to changes in the marketplace very quickly. There will always be a market for good ideas. The conference market might dry up, the multimedia market might dry up, we might all get bored with the Internet and 'get real' rather than 'go virtual', but whatever the media and marketing mix, there will always be the need for good ideas. We live for the idea. We have all of the necessary strategic, creative, planning, logistics, technical and production management resources here to have ideas and make them happen but, at the end of the day, we want to talk to visionary brand owners about doing visionary things. Some people think we're mad, others think we're arrogant; I believe we have integrity. We know what we can do and where we are going, and we are committed to building relationships with people who are going to enjoy working with us.

THE JENKINS GROUP, LONDON, UK
Nicholas Jenkins

- Business development from existing clients is cheap. The sales costs are almost nil.

I have a new marketing plan: I am going to change my name by deed poll to Terence Conran, as he is the only designer anyone's ever heard of.

The Jenkins Group has a formal marketing structure. We have a Marketing Director who is responsible for a group of marketing people, each targeting one of our key sectors of packaging, interiors and corporate identity. These people are in turn backed up by account managers. One of their tasks is to read the papers for an hour or so every morning to source information and obtain leads. About 15 per cent of our business comes through this method – the rest comes from other sources, particularly the development of existing business, for example the WH Smith business, on which we worked for 15 years, and on whose business our company was really founded.

What else would I suggest? Keep raising the profile – accept all invitations to speak on panels; at about one out of eight evening events you meet the right guy. Also, be opportunistic. Think laterally. For example, I once wrote to the Archbishop of Canterbury, whose offices are next to ours in Westminster, and we are now doing a lot of work for the Church of England. Another example: a large company in Dubai rang and asked The Jenkins Group to present our credentials on an all-expenses paid trip. We went, pitched, but lost the job to Landor. However, we had flown out on a deal where we got an extra free ticket, and we got the Marketing Director to fix up ten appointments. From that came three jobs.

As far as working in other countries is concerned, we have two companies in Spain as connecting pipelines – a management consultancy and an artwork company. If you do not have connections like these, the cost of working abroad is prohibitive, because of all of the travelling. As a result, we tend to only work in the UK, in Dubai and in Spain.

It's also important to get to know people. PR people are brilliant; we got a big piece of work because we knew the right PR guy. Also clients moving on to another company can be a terrific source of business. Who else? The Royal Family can also be quite useful – we got a couple of exhibitions because of them.

KINNEIR DUFORT DESIGN, BRISTOL, UK

Ross Kinneir

- At first meetings, we use our portfolio selectively. For example, we don't show milk bottles to a telephone manufacturer; it is just a waste of time.

When I started, it was a real Catch-22 situation. Clients were not interested in giving you your first freelance job until you could prove that you had successfully completed your first freelance job. You just had to be prepared to tell a few white lies and really dig in. Now it is quite the opposite. We show our work and say: 'This is what we have done; we can do the same for you.' We find that it's best just to say 'Come and have a look,' instead of wading in with long sentences about our strategic ability. We use their language, and if we were talking to a manufacturer of asthma inhalers, we would show them something vaguely medical rather than a bicycle pump.

Of course, there are times when you have to be prepared for companies to ask why they should use you when you have never designed a product like theirs before. We look them in the eye and say that although we haven't designed anything exactly like theirs before, we are able to solve their problem by using our analytical and creative talents. In one instance, we took letters of reference with us to the meeting and said that although we had never worked on pharmaceutical products such as theirs, we had equally never worked on a virtual reality computer before the one we had just successfully designed, and we showed them the letters as proof of the results. It gives the clients confidence, but it does depend on the personality of the client, and how willing he or she is to move away from the well-trodden footpath.

We tend not to approach companies where we will simply be put in a long queue of designers. Usually, this means not contacting the known names, where there is bound to be a queue, or those who have specific design buyers or design managers. Clients like these are bound to have a pile of unread brochures on their desk or in the bin. We write to people with a specific offer of our expertise in their field. We like the idea of being seen as being confident in projects which involve new technology; it puts us into a different category. It is too easy for designers to be seen as generalists, and I feel that it is important to project ourselves as real specialists. It allows us to talk to focused clients, who know what they want to do.

Although I do most of the new business marketing, our success depends very much on the efforts of the whole team at Kinneir Dufort. For instance, I know that while I am pursuing one lead, my co-director Jim Orkney can be finalizing another and making sure that our designers and modelmakers are briefed and ready to begin any new work. Similarly, the designers themselves are alert to new business opportunities and the all-important development of existing client relationships. The test of a good client relationship is who a client asks for when they phone. Clients can be wary of being passed down the line, but I always tell them that the reason we are a successful team is that we have such a spread of talents.

We don't follow any rules, although our general pattern is to write a letter and follow it up with a phone call. That's what I expect from people trying to sell to me; you should be able to put your offer into 15 to 20 lines or so. If you phone first, instead of writing, you can be treated with some suspicion. How does the person at the other end know that you are not an industrial spy? Confidentiality is vital in the world of industrial design. If you send a letter and brochure first, they will be reassured that you are who you say you are.

The great difficulty is knowing where a given company is on its product development cycle. You have a wait of unknown length for a window of opportunity, and then when the window does come it might only be four days long with the client in a last-minute rush, so you can easily miss it. You've got to register in their consciousness. I always say that there are four hurdles to overcome: first, find the right person; next, make sure that they hear what you say, listen and understand; third, hope that they remember your name when the time comes; and last, be able to find your name and telephone number. We have made sure that our brochure will be passed from the secretary to the boss, and not put in the bin immediately, and that the boss will think that it is so good that he or she does not want to throw it away either. Our brochure is designed to be tactile, to be visual and have a perceived quality. It also fits a standard filing cabinet or shelf, so that they can find it again. This is all in order to register with that person, and to have something memorable to talk about when we phone. It works.

Having said all of that, some of the best jobs we have had come through the most convoluted introductions. We also proposition companies. By this, I mean that we go to them with an idea and make them realize that we have something to offer. We designed the AA roadside telephones as a result of a direct written proposal to the Chairman, and we wrote to the BBC and proposed that we should design a new technology RDS radio. In both cases, intelligent persistence resulted in a significant commission, with no investment of time up front on our part. The designing didn't start until we were being paid fees. People now accept that our pro-active stance yields results and our profile is greatly enhanced.

LANDOR ASSOCIATES, LONDON, UK

Peter Farnell-Watson

- We prefer to have relationships with our clients, rather than projects from them.

There are two groups of people involved in our marketing programme. One group consists of people who are sector experts – for example in the pharmaceutical, financial services or telecommunications businesses – who follow developments in those sectors across Europe, and then put together marketing plans. We have selected seven key sectors where there are significant opportunities for us. The other group of people covers our main geographical markets in Europe and Africa. If a sector expert and a geographical expert spot the same opportunity, they go in together, and that means that we combine someone with local knowledge – both commercial and cultural – with someone who is experienced in that particular industry. The people who develop the business then manage the business. It really is teamwork. As we evolve, we are becoming much more matrix-management based in terms of people working together, and that philosophy goes right across our organization.

We believe that the way forward for us is through our expertise. The market is getting more and more knowledgeable, and if we approach potential clients as a generalist, it's not going to wash. It's far better to have people who know what's going on in a specific industry, particularly when dealing with the kind of work we are doing, which involves top level strategic input. You can't just mumble your way through it.

Of course, we have roll-over work from year to year; we are in corporate and brand identity and retail, and some of our work involves long-term projects. For example, an airline project goes on for a long time, whereas some packaging work happens very quickly. Clearly, what we are trying to do – and I think everybody else is trying to do the same thing – is to develop longer-term relationships with major clients. Clients are beginning to see the advantage of this, even in the corporate identity field.

In terms of getting our name known, we have been fairly quiet over the years, and it is only recently that we have hired a full-time communications director to look after Landor in Europe. We are trying to build a profile not only in the UK but also in other major markets: France, Italy, Spain, Germany and the Nordic countries. The PR programme becomes multi-dimensional. As we are working to raise our profile both in geographical markets, and also in our chosen sectors, it is very important that our sector experts and our geographical experts work very closely with our communications director.

Landor has more complicated communication issues to address than many design companies because we are so international – simple things like language, for example. The company itself is evolving to a point where each region does its own communications, and does not rely on material produced elsewhere, such as in America. For us to be appropriate in our own market, we have to be seen as Europeans, but as a European component of a global company. After all, that is our advantage compared with other design companies. Worldwide, Landor has clear communication guidelines – with a core mission and a core positioning – and it's important that in Europe we don't give out a different message from what is going on in the States or the Far East. However, there are certain things which we do in Europe which are unique to this market and which, far from affecting the notion of what the brand is, support the brand.

With the advances in electronics and developments like the Internet, working across borders becomes seamless, and you don't necessarily need an office or a studio on the ground to reach the major markets. The way we manage our business and handle our clients is changing dramatically. For example, you have to decide when you are going to do things from a distance, and when you need to have people in the same room.

As a large company, we also have to make sure that we keep communicating with each other. Every year we have a worldwide meeting, and in addition to that there are sessions involving key people across the organization, with regular meetings for the financial group, managing directors' group, creative group, and so on. We also have meetings about our practices, such as corporate identity, branding, and naming. Together, we build knowledge, and try to make sure we don't reinvent the wheel.

My advice to other companies – and I think that it's pretty straightforward – is to be focused. You have to be very specific about what you are trying to do, and you've got to put whatever funds you have available behind that one thing. The design industry is getting more and more fragmented; a lot of people are coming into our business, and a lot of us are getting into related businesses as well. The picture is getting blurred, and that means that your offer has got to be absolutely clear. Certainly, the clients that we see are beginning to look for ongoing communications and marketing relationships, not only in the field of design but also, in a wider context, in an integrated range of services. In the future, companies are going to have to form strategic relationships or partnerships with others in order to enhance their own product and put together an appropriate package to get the business.

LEWIS MOBERLY, LONDON, UK
Robert Moberly

- I use the analogy that creativity is the power of the gun, and strategic skills are the ability to hit the target. One without the other is useless; you must have both.

We have been very lucky. Before starting our company, I had worked in advertising and Mary Lewis had a broader experience as fine art printmaker, art school lecturer and freelance designer. We had collaborated on several projects, for example Bass, and most of our contacts gave us work. My agency contacts were very supportive, and clients in that first year included ICI Dulux, Bass, Heinz and Shippams. We focused on our product rather than marketing ourselves. We were dedicated to our creative output and profile and we never took on more people than we needed. One client simply led to another at a controlled pace. Clients like Johnson & Johnson have been with us since those early days. Repeat business is very important to us, as is the spread and variety of our business.

Perhaps this has made us a little less sharp than we should have been in marketing ourselves. We believe that cold calling is the wrong way to begin a relationship and mass mailings end up in the bin. We did embark on a short advertising campaign to coincide with our tenth anniversary but, although two resulting client projects more than paid for it, we wouldn't recommend advertising either. It came out in *Marketing Week* on the very day, as it happened, that I was speaking at one of their conferences. There was a copy on everyone's desk, and our advertisement was on the first double page spread, inside the front cover. I watched as people flicked through. They turned over the pages in less than a second, unless there was a compelling reason to stop. What I quickly realized was that everyone there who worked for a design company spent time reading our advertisement, and everyone who worked for a client company didn't. Advertising only connects if someone has an interest in the subject in the first place, and clients are not intrinsically interested in design; they simply don't go around all the time feeling that they need it. When they see an advertisement, they don't immediately think 'Ah, good! Here's a design company,' they just turn the page.

There is no doubt that the most important way of building a business is to start with a few contacts, and then really keep in touch with those people, the people you know, the people you've worked with. Start building up this body of people who have experienced your brand, and keep them constantly aware of what you're doing, even when they've gone on to do other things. You should never think: 'In that job they'll never buy design.' That's quite irrelevant. You are in the business of building *relationships* with people who are going to go on rising up through their organizations. You do this by keeping in touch with them, by making sure you've got a very good mailing list, and by writing personal notes to them, not great big mailers. Remind them of the time when you worked together, and keep it on a very personal level. Occasionally, of course, you might invite them to something. For example, if you've done some revolutionary thinking about how design works, you might put together a seminar and send invitations to these people, the people you've always known.

Word of mouth is by far the most powerful advertising medium, and anything you can do to encourage it is going to work for you. That is where PR comes in. We haven't made a huge effort in PR, which we have managed both in-house and externally, but we do cultivate the press, and let them know if we have interesting things to say. It's a relatively low-level campaign but it's very valuable.

We don't do anything specific for overseas markets as they are far too big to tackle well, although we do have an agent in Spain. We tend instead to rely on word of mouth, just as we do in the UK. We have been published, for example, in a German marketing magazine which approached us saying that they would like to do an article on Lewis Moberly. We are sent briefs from Japan, America and several European countries. This situation has arisen from a combination of our general reputation and the fact that our work is published in books which circulate in the international community.

We have won a lot of awards for our work. We have hundreds of them, we have rooms full of them, we hide some of them because they are so ugly. The whole issue of winning creative awards is a double-edged sword of course, because clients might say: 'Oh, that's all they're interested in, they do that for themselves.' There is, however, a direct client benefit. It means that the talent – particularly the new, young talent – wants to come and work here; we have first access to the talent stream. That is certainly in the clients' interest, as is that little bit of adrenalin it gives to the whole of our organization. Of course, any creativity which is undirected towards a commercial goal is of no value to the client whatsoever, and so we have built our business on two pillars, one being creative and the other strategic. We win design effectiveness awards as well as creative awards, and we have been either a finalist or a winner every year the DBA Design Effectiveness Awards have run. We are very proud of that.

The advice I would give to newer design companies is that it's always best to start in a small way, and develop relationships. But they've got to invest. For example, they might take a market area where they think that the design isn't very good, and do some research in order to go to a potential client with a point of view. It demonstrates that they've really shown a level of interest, that their brains have engaged on a problem. It is possible to come up with insights that the client might not have thought of; not about the market itself but about how design is working or not working in that market. At Lewis Moberly, we spend a great deal of time thinking about our clients' businesses. We will never do free creative pitches – we are very firm about that – but I think that clients have every right to see our brains engaged on their specific problems before they appoint us.

Mary would add that her personal goal is to win Design Effectiveness Awards with work that has also won the creative awards. She has done this consistently, supporting our view that creativity and effectiveness are not mutually exclusive, but at their most potent as one.

LLOYD NORTHOVER CITIGATE, LONDON, UK

Jim Northover

- We try to get into conversation with potential clients rather than just go for one pitch after another. The project itself should not be the main emphasis; it should be the relationship.

As we see it, marketing is about understanding the skills that we have, knowing who needs them, and then adapting the one to fit the other. It all sounds very straightforward, but it is the basis on which we work. It's not just a sales job.

We have been in business for over 20 years and, in many ways, what we do now is the same as we have always done, but it's all much bigger. For example, we rely on a better database of information and a wider range of contacts than we had on Day One. One thing we did in the early days when we were a little more naive was to try to persuade people over the telephone: we don't even think about doing that now. We try to engage potential clients in a conversation, which means listening to them, talking about their business and the issues that are important for them, and about the contribution we can make. We look for particular insights, and then point them out. Those kinds of conversations tend to lead somewhere – not necessarily to immediate work, but to the kind of relationship where a potential client can talk to you about something even if there is not a job in the offing.

We run a team approach to marketing. All of the directors here are designers in their own right, and we are all involved in some way in marketing or business generation. We also have a dedicated marketing unit, whose job it is to ensure that everything is kept on track and that progress is monitored. They give professional advice on both the strategy and tactics of marketing. We don't have account managers; we have designers, consultants, researchers and project coordinators. Those individuals are the main converters of new business, and we think that it is vital to include in the pitch the people who will be working on the project. They also have the responsibility for maintaining the relationship once the business has been won. We try to act as a team, rather than a bunch of separate individuals. It's always a balance between our corporate style and our very diverse personalities.

We keep our approach as human as we can, and try to be light on our feet. We don't have stock proposals or stock responses to a project, but keep everything tailor-made to the individual client enquiry. This means that we sometimes reinvent wheels, but we don't like a formulaic approach.

We try to keep in regular contact with our potential client base, and we do that in whatever way seems to be appropriate. We write to people. The cold letter is inevitably rather difficult, so you've got to have something compelling to say. If an industry sector is going through a period of change, we might raise some of the key issues with companies in that sector to see if we can strike a chord.

We try to meet people at all sorts of opportunities. Ideally, we would spend more time networking, establishing contacts and meeting people through other people. Periodically, we might host informal lunches for clients to debate relevant topics, but we don't tend to take people to the opera or a test match or whatever – we don't find that as useful as just conversing with them. Informal, direct, professional: that's what we go for.

We are long-term believers in PR and in regular communication. As an example, we have been running a newsletter for over 15 years, and have published 20 issues during that period, with one name change. It has been irregular in the times it has come out, but it's been there, it has kept on coming out. Our PR has historically been done in-house, but we are now working with two colleagues at Citigate who help us with fresh ideas and share the workload. They also make sure that some of the activities just get done.

We have an extensive brochure about our work in the two decades we've been going, and this is our third major publication. We occasionally make videos about our work or about our participation with our clients, so it becomes a mini-showreel of our activities, particularly on more involved communication programmes. We have a new media unit comprising five or six members of staff whose job it is to review all new developments in media, and we have something about ourselves on the Web, and shortly on CD-ROM.

We have offices in Asia, the Middle East, South Africa and North America; some as partner companies, some joint ventures, some wholly owned. The design work is done both in London and locally. We don't see ourselves as exporting, or as doing work overseas. It's one world, and we are one company with people living and working in different places. We are very much against making a distinction between what's UK and what isn't – it's totally artificial. For global clients, who might have a head office in one country and the majority of their market in another, the concept of territorial origin no longer makes any sense. For client companies operating in the UK only, any international expertise we have can only come as an advantage. They need to benchmark themselves against the best in the world.

We are keen to retain our clients. The link might be with a company or with a person, both are important. We've got one or two client companies who have been with us for 20 years, others for ten years. We have worked with one person on major projects in five separate companies. The way we do it is to keep the dialogue going. We continue to provide any new insights we can, and we take a real interest in our clients' businesses. We try to establish a basis of trust: it's so important, but it has become rather undervalued. Long term, mutual trust between a design company and a client is vital.

What advice would I give to any young people starting their own company? If they are certain that they want to be their own boss, if they really have to do it, and can see no other way forward, then they should do it – that's how it was for me. They will need to ask themselves whether they are prepared for the risks as well as the rewards. Of course, in a way you can't answer those questions when you start up, until you've been there and done it, but they are worth thinking about.

Firstly, listen carefully and learn about clients' businesses. I've learnt nearly everything I know about business and about managing people from the clients I've worked with, in addition to my own experience and reading. Having worked with some of the brightest and most respected CEOs and senior managers, I've learnt a lot from them about how to get messages across and how to work with them rather than for them. Secondly, be yourself rather than adopt some preconceived notion of what marketing is all about. Your individual personality and qualities are what the best kind of clients are looking for. Lastly, never promise what you can't deliver, but always deliver what you promise. Be consistent, deliver high-quality design, year in and year out. It sounds boring, but that's what makes a strong business. Bright fireworks are great, but it's consistency and sustainability that make really good, enduring design companies.

MILLFORD-VAN DEN BERG DESIGN, WASSENAAR, HOLLAND
Jan Oldenburger

- The way we reach new clients is through our existing clients. When we do excellent work for them, they spread the news; they are ambassadors for us. The only dangerous thing is that our clients might want to keep us for themselves, as a hidden secret.

We have a very simple new business plan: we do the best possible work for our existing clients. We always say that the supermarket is our permanent exhibition. So that's the first thing that we do: the second is that we do a lot of training programmes for existing clients. This can develop into something on quite a large scale. For example, we work for several divisions of Unilever, and over the last four years we have become an important part of the Unilever training programme for their marketing people. Every year, we talk to 20 or so product managers who have about two years experience, and who work in different Unilever divisions. We also do this for Sara Lee, and a number of big Dutch companies. We teach them about packaging design and its role within the marketing and communication mix, and we do case studies on working procedures. We don't talk about the end results or how good our work is, since they can see that in the supermarket, but about how difficult and how important the design process is. These two methods – good work and training programmes – are the strongest ways of creating business for us.

We also go to a lot of conferences on marketing and advertising and so on, and we participate by giving speeches and even designing conference logos. We work hard on our spontaneous brand awareness: I want to be top-of-mind, so that when someone thinks about packaging design they think of Millford first (or second or third, but that's it – no lower).

We work mostly for clients based in the Netherlands, but they are from international organizations; we know that local markets will increasingly be managed internationally. That is why we are so active in design organizations such as the PDA [Pan-European Brands Design Association], and why we have established our own business network across Europe with design companies in Düsseldorf, Milan, London, Paris and Denmark.

In a way, we are a bit conservative; we expand internationally little by little from our existing client base. We don't want to grow too quickly because we want to retain our quality. We don't want to have a second Millford-van den Berg Design in Germany or wherever. We want to have one company, and to grow in quality, not in quantity.

We manage our customer care programme by working hard and producing good work, by taking initiatives and surprising them. And, of course, we do the training programmes – and we don't charge them for the training, it's all free.

Little by little, we are being considered not as a design company but as partners. We get involved in many aspects of our clients' businesses, even advising on which advertising agency to select and helping them to define positioning statements for their brands. We have moved into our clients' companies on a very deep level, and we have worked for some of our clients for many years.

I do not cold call any of my design company colleagues' existing clients. We have never done it. If a potential client is already doing good design work, I would not go in there to ask for work. In Holland, we are a little bit strict about that. Clients sometimes call to discuss a project with us because my partners and I are really well known in the communication world, and when work comes to us, it is 90 per cent on the client's initiative.

It always seems as though you should have a big plan, but the best thing we have to show is ourselves. What clients buy in the end is people, and the only thing we have to sell is creativity and people. If clients like us, they will come to us. If they don't, they will never come, no matter how professional we are. We do excellent work and we are very enthusiastic, but also a little bit aggressive and outspoken. Clients tend to fall in love with us, or not. They know that we really like the work we are doing, and they know that there are no false pretences. When you reach that point, you don't need to write or call them.

MINALE TATTERSFIELD, RICHMOND, UK

Marcello Minale

● How have we achieved our success? Well, I am glad to say that it has not been through marketing. We are a design-led company, of which there are probably only two or three on Planet Earth. All of the others are slowly pursuing a marketing-led course. I know that my point of view has always been controversial, but I am violently against anything called 'marketing'.

Minale Tattersfield was established in 1964 and now has operating offices in 13 different countries including Australia, Japan, Kuwait, Hong Kong, Kuala Lumpur and all of Europe. In financial terms, we are probably ranked at number three or four internationally, but I am arrogant enough to believe that as a worldwide network we are number one. This success cannot be achieved in a short time: we have pursued a long-term programme for well over 30 years.

Our way of selling ourselves is completely different from other design consultancies. Our success is based on the idea that you have to generate the contact that comes to you, and you do not go to the contact. Our principle is that the mountain comes to Mohammed – Mohammed does not go to the mountain.

First, you have to produce jobs which are interesting enough to create enough publicity in the design press. We got well known in the first place by doing good work which people talked about. When you produce a revolutionary job, as we did even 30 years ago, the ball runs by itself.

Second, it is important to have international recognition, to be perceived to have an international language. In doing this, you create a chain reaction. For example, we have been invited by various official bodies to take part in their activities. Twenty years ago, we started a travelling exhibition about our work and related cultural aspects, and it has been updated ever since. This has now gone from the Design Council in London to Madrid, Milan, Tokyo and Mexico City. The exhibition is always by invitation and, luckily, paid for by the sponsors. It has been visited by an average of between 50 000 and 60 000 people in every place it has been: this obviously generates contacts. However, it is not much use producing an exhibition of your work unless people want it. It would defeat the object and become just a marketing thing.

Another aspect is the publication of our books; once someone has bought a book, there is a chance that they will be interested in reading it. Again, you have to produce jobs interesting enough for publishers to make the required investment. We have been lucky, and have published six books to date about our work. All of these are published in different languages: for example, the second edition of *How To Run a Successful Multi-Disciplinary Design Company* will be translated into Chinese, and will be one of the few Chinese books on design.

We have sold an average of 10 000 copies per book, so we've got 60 000 books around the world. This basically generates five contacts every month, from a completely international audience, who feel that the jobs they have seen are just the kind of solutions they require for their own specific projects.

We have a core of clients who have been with us for 20 to 25 years. We change the team every two or three years to keep the thinking fresh. Often, the relationship between a designer and a client can deteriorate with too much familiarity; here, this doesn't happen.

Cold calling, credentials presentations and so on are a complete waste of time. This kind of marketing has been the cancer of our industry, which no longer 'does', but which merely talks of doing it. Very small amounts of jobs are done, but a massive amount of talking about jobs takes place. You find yourself in a competition where a job doesn't exist, but where for six months you investigate that job which never will happen. This is the industry today; it is a fact.

The doom of death is writing a letter, that I can vouch for. You never employ consultants that write to you, whether they are accountants, solicitors or whatever – by nature, it is not an ethical gesture to make. If you go to a company, you are immediately seen as being part of a profession which writes and you are in a weak position. If a company comes to you, you are in a strong position. We are lucky to have enough enquiries that we do not need to approach companies which do not want us, or companies where we have to prove ourselves. It's too great a dispersal of energy. The proof of the pudding is that every company which has persisted in cold calling has gone bust, because the effort was too great.

I would advise newcomers to specialize, to corner a small part of a big market and become an expert in that area. That's the only future for design. People have to want you, there must be a reason for appointing you, and the best reason is that you are a specialist. If you can design coupons with the best response mechanisms ever, then you should do just that. I can guarantee that there are enough people needing coupons to fill a building.

PI DESIGN INTERNATIONAL, LONDON, UK
Chris Griffin

- The key to successful marketing – and it's only something that we have been able to crack in the last three years or so – is that marketing has to be inside every single employee.

Originally, having launched the company on the back of our expertise gained at Metalbox, we were the only structural packaging design company in Europe. Shortly afterwards, we extended into packaging graphics. The company is still positioned single-mindedly in packaging design, specifically branded packaging design. We do not work for retailers, as they currently have a different and conflicting approach to brands.

How do we market ourselves? Every discipline within our business has got a client orientation and that has to do both with the people and the culture. It means looking outside the company, but also it means looking inside, looking at the product we are delivering. Developing a product to meet the consumers' needs, also in our case the clients' needs, is after all part of the definition of marketing.

The way we've done it is by recruiting people who have both an internal and an external focus. All of our marketeers, for example, work on new business as well as ongoing projects. I have observed that a number of other companies seem to have one team focused on external issues and one on internal, and I think that it builds tension and prevents the company culture moving in the right direction. A little internal friction can be a good thing, but it's important to get the balance right. It has to be a positive force, one that delivers an improved proposition to the client.

After 12 years, a lot of our work is repeat business, and doing good design work is clearly the root of successful client development. We still need to approach new clients, and we probably use almost every technique in the book. The only one we don't major on is picking up magazines, seeing what the issues are, and ringing up the potential client. We don't wait for the stimulation of the article. Generally, we might approach a potential client by sending a letter suggesting that we have some thoughts about their brand gained from our experience in their own or comparable markets. It could be about structural or graphic packaging, brand analysis, profitability or environmental issues. There are a whole range of topics depending on the person or company we are targeting. It doesn't take very long, given the way we work, to come up with the most relevant issues or areas of interest. It's just bubbling away top-of-mind all the time. We speak at conferences, we commission research, and I do a lot of work with the Marketing Society, which I suppose is another route to awareness. We do PR, but not as much in the last couple of years as perhaps we should.

Our work outside the UK accounts for over 60 per cent of our business. We have had an office in Brussels since 1990, with designers but no sales people; we handle that side of things from London. We market ourselves to international clients in exactly the same way as to UK clients, in a worldwide programme. The real frustration in this country is the UK-ness of everything. Nobody's forming alliances overseas, nobody's pushing Europe, and yet more and more of our clients have got a European or global presence.

We have formed an association with the US design consultancy Libby Perszyk Kathman because more and more of our clients have been moving from a European to a global agenda. We've observed too many design companies fail to set up on their own in the States; some have made it, but most have caught a slight sniffle if not a cold. We decided to tackle it through association, and what we found in LPK – after a search of three or four years – was a cultural link that we felt could work. The more we progress, the more we discover that we are covering the same issues and pursuing things in the same way. Similarly, LPK were understandably apprehensive about working in Europe. How could they cope with all of these small countries and different languages and cultures? They knew that they couldn't just go in and do it the American way, but had to do it differently. It's been a good move for both of us.

In late 1995, we relaunched the company to mark our management buyout and US association. We introduced a new corporate identity with a teaser campaign on anonymous postcards, held a media conference with our American colleagues from LPK present, threw a terrific party for clients in Planet Hollywood, and sent a roving squad out overnight to put blue, white and red balloons – the three colours of our logo – outside the offices of clients, media and some of our competitors. It was very unusual for us to do something like that, and it worked. It left a really strong impression. It took a lot of resource, a lot of time, a lot of money and it's only something you do when you've got something special to mark.

We will not free pitch, ever. Our answer is always a flat, categorical, absolute 'No'. In fact, we have persuaded clients who have asked us to free pitch to pay a fee, by using the arguments from the DBA booklet together with our own arguments about the danger to the market of free pitching. I get very, very angry about free pitches especially when, as happened recently, a major brand at nearly the hundred million mark comes along saying we want to do really strategic work and the first creative stage will be for nothing. It's an absolute joke and brands which behave like this deserve to die at the hands of own label. Good luck to the retailers, I say. We are always paid fees for competitive pitches, although we occasionally reduce our usual fees slightly if the target client offers strategic opportunities for the future. However, we also negotiate terms of business to run alongside any less than 100 per cent recovery pitches, whereby if the work proceeds, the client makes good the rest of the fee and owns the work. Otherwise, we own it.

PINEAPPLE DESIGN, BRUSSELS, BELGIUM

Rowland Heming

- What do we do to retain our clients? We bend over backwards. Seriously, the simple answer is that we just care. We keep them informed all of the time, and let them know that we are thinking about them.

My wife, Bridgid, and I trained in the UK. I then worked for Bowater Packaging, Metalbox and British Cellophane before deciding to join the American company Cato Johnson in Belgium in 1974. After five years or so, I realized that at that time there was no real competition in Belgium and that there was an opportunity for someone else to start up. As it happened, although I didn't know it then, three or four other design groups launched at the same time. After a while working on a freelance basis, and a brief time in Hong Kong, re-employed by Cato Johnson, Bridgid and I really woke up to what we should be doing, and on returning to Brussels, changed from a freelance house to a design company overnight.

In the initial stages we only marketed ourselves to the clients that we had. In other words, we moved more broadly within each of our clients' companies. That went on for about five years, and every year Pineapple Design doubled in size. However, the recession then hit us, and we had to re-address everything. We reduced the company in size, and although we kept our office in Portugal, we closed our other offices across Europe. Now, however, we are almost back to our previous strength again.

What works for us in marketing? One thing that doesn't work is advertising. It costs a fortune, and nobody really sees it; in our business nobody responds to advertisements in that way. The most that you can hope for is that someone might say; 'Oh yes, I've heard of them', but that's about it. I know that PR works, but we don't do a lot of it: we don't really go in for a lot of show. What does work for us is direct contact. Over the years we have used different methods, and the telephone is probably the best. At first, we had a very simple system. We would call, and if they were interested we would take it further. If they said 'No', we would ask if we could send our brochure, and then call them and ask if they received it. In this way you have two or three chances to get somewhere with them.

Since that simple beginning, we have developed a completely different strategy, and that is one of total support. Once we have identified a client and have got past the talking stage, we ask them to one of our workshops. We run these for potential clients and also for the large marketing colleges, so that we start to build a reputation with people who will become marketing directors in the future. We invite people from different companies to our offices, and occasionally mix in some of our existing clients as well. The workshops last a full morning, and cover the management of packaging design. We go through the how and why of packaging, discuss retail issues, and show how to build a brand and ensure that it continues to work over the years.

We follow up the workshops with continuous support. If we see articles which are interesting, we copy them to the people who have been along to our workshops. If we do anything new, we let them know. For example, we had two students from a marketing college here for three months doing a thesis on own-brand packaging; that gave rise to mailings. The other thing we do is a course of lectures on subjects related to our profession, for example on packaging design research. We try to keep potential clients thinking that we care about them, even if they are not yet our clients.

All of this is done for free. However, we will not free pitch. Once someone asks us to do something, we will charge a fee. We believe that working for nothing devalues what we do for our loyal clients, who value our work and who pay for it.

We also offer to evaluate packaging from a design point of view. It's not research; it's a designer looking at it from the outside. Whereas a consumer might say 'I like it' or 'I don't like it', we would say 'It works (or it doesn't work) because…' We charge a fee for this consultancy work, and we offer it to everyone, not just our clients. It's part of gaining their confidence, of building up our reputation of quality, of being seen to be a professional company.

We are a Ministry-approved design consultancy. The Ministère de la Wallonie offers grants to client companies to do their packaging and, once they receive an application, the Ministry appoints a consultancy such as ours to judge whether what the client is asking for is realistic and affordable. We would submit a report, for which we are paid a set fee, and if the client company is successful, they are told to ask three Ministry-approved design companies to quote for the work. It is then up to the client to decide who they appoint. The Ministry will pay something like two thirds of the cost.

We used to market ourselves only to international companies, but with the recession we realized we had to be a bit cleverer than that. At Pineapple, we had a particularly heavy recession as it affected US companies badly, and these mostly formed the base of our business. We now have a twin-track strategy, where we can sit with the biggest companies and talk in terms that they will understand, but we have also learned to attune our language to companies who would be frightened to death if you talked to them in the same language. We have made a lot of effort to reach the PMEs [Petites Moyennes Entreprises] or small-to-medium businesses. For example, we publish articles in their own magazine, the PME, on how to protect brands and so on. We have addressed ourselves to that scale of business.

There is an important difference between national and international design. Designers who work for a national market tend to think about that market and how design has evolved. The British market, for example, is quite well developed; others are much less so. National designers tend to produce images in their own national style. International designers tend to look at it differently. We don't try to impose a style on the country we are working for. Instead, we try to understand the style of that country and design for that style. It's a subtle difference, but it's what makes an international design group successful.

We care for our clients, and we want to retain them. If we go in for any awards, we do it together with our clients – they like to have them. Also, in recent years, we have tried to develop much more transparent costings and pricing, which isn't as easily done as said. Nevertheless, we are trying our best to achieve it. Why? Because it makes our clients happy, and that's good for business.

SAMPSON TYRRELL, LONDON, UK
Dave Allen

- It's almost as if our competitors assume that projects are going to stop, and so they do. We are the complete reverse: we assume that they are never going to stop, and so they don't. They become programmes.

Eight or ten years back, we decided who we wanted to sell our services to, and what we wanted to sell them. We decided that we wanted to become Europe's leading identity company, and that we wanted to become a key advisor to the world's best corporations. We have been single-mindedly working on that objective since, and everything we do is measured against it. There are 500 companies whom we target, mostly in Europe. When we started the process, nobody had ever heard of us; now we are in regular contact with all of those companies and talk to them three or four times a year, either by phone or by going to see them. We now have a database of all of the people we need to talk to in those 500 companies, and that obviously takes a long time to build up.

We have a dedicated marketing team, with a full-time director, manager and assistant, and also telemarketing and database managers. This team does not get involved in any ongoing consultancy; it markets the business. It creates the best environment for our consultants – our sales people – to function effectively in. It makes sure that people are aware of the company and what we do and, as a support to that, it follows up with work in specific sectors. For example, we may do a study of the car industry, and then we would target, say, ten large car companies. The marketing team would approach the company, and then once an appointment had been made, our consultants would take over.

Our brochures set standards. We place a lot of emphasis on them, and they have been incredibly useful to us. When we were embarking on this approach in the late 1980s, we did some research and found that design was not seen as a strategic service, but as a tactical tool, so we created the term Visual Management, which is now trademarked across Europe to protect it. We then produced our book on Visual Management, which proved to be a stepping stone to becoming a consultancy which puts visual identity in its proper context, as part of a broader consultancy offering. If you are an identity consultancy, the assumption is that you do logos when obviously you do an awful lot more. As a part of our service, Visual Management offers the management of a client's identity on a national or international basis. That's one of the ways in which we have been able to move from having identity projects to identity programmes, almost amounting to a retained advisory service.

Out of everything, I suppose PR is the one thing we have not put much effort into, but that's not because I think it doesn't work. I am a great believer in the simple premise that the more someone hears about you in different contexts, the better. You need to write to them, they need to see an ad, they need to hear you talked about at some sort of function, and to see your name in the press. We currently subcontract PR. We've tried both internal and external methods, and have always found it a difficult area. It's hard to find a good commercially-oriented PR person, someone who can explain to the business community what identity can do for business in a way that gets the press interested. The media always seem to take it down to crass ideas, for example looking at the logos of the Royal Family. You just cringe and think 'Here we go again.' What we did not want was to be compartmentalized among the design industry, because we knew that took us down into Logoland, so we took the decision to keep out of the press.

We also did not want to have an identified guru inside the business. We decided eight years ago that to have the equivalent of a Wally Olins or a Michael Peters was a disadvantage, because people come in and expect to see them. If we are going to develop a strong business, what clients should be buying is Sampson Tyrrell, not Dave Allen. That makes it far more difficult; it would be much easier to promote myself and what I think than what Sampson Tyrrell thinks, which is much less personal.

In a way, we have been quite cautious about saying what we are doing – I am very wary of plagiarism in the design business. We keep our secrets very close to our chest. We prefer to send information to client prospects to intrigue them to come in here, and then we explain what we do. The problem is, half the client work we do is so confidential that we can't talk about it, which can make things difficult.

In terms of building long-term relationships with our clients, we have people in the consultancy who are from very different backgrounds, such as identity experts, branding experts, internal communications people and behavioural psychologists. We also have an extensive training programme to keep people abreast of new ideas and developments. People here are encouraged to put ideas forward to clients. Once you are working at a senior corporate level, you can stretch an identity project into a programme so that it is almost continuous. If you can't do that, you can provide your clients with other good ideas. As a result of that, we've probably done better than anybody in terms of keeping relationships with our clients for far, far longer than would be normal for an identity company.

We don't have satellite offices abroad, and we don't use overseas agents. We have a global network of one office. I would regard the decision made in the 1980s not to open foreign offices as one of my better ones. We did a few experiments, and proved that even if you have an office in Milan, people in Italy think that London is the centre for international graphic design, and the amounts of money you can charge in London are far greater than if you were in Italy. Also, if you're targeting the top 500, and you've done a project in Portugal, there's as much chance of business coming from Finland as from Portugal. It's no problem to be based in London; we often have up to ten people somewhere in Europe or the Middle East or Asia in any one given week. You can do a day trip to just about anywhere in Europe now.

Marketing can never be a substitute for selling, because selling is a separate skill. I sometimes think that one of the reasons we have been so successful is that our competitors are so bad at it. Marketing is about making people aware and creating the environment, creating desire. Selling is about explaining to that person that you are the right people to fulfil that desire. When it comes to a service company, it is important for anyone setting up in this business to separate marketing and selling in their heads. So many people I meet are totally confused; they create a new business team who are supposed to do marketing and selling – and who in practice don't do much of either. They do a bit of PR to get a few enquiries, then they go off and try to do some selling. Usually, they are pretty bad at selling; they just tell people what they've got, rather than listening to what they need.

If there is one area where the design industry needs to improve enormously it is in our ability to explain what it is that we all do and translate that into something which will benefit the client. Marketing alone can't do that; you have to have human interaction. You can send out brochures and write ads until you are blue in the face, but it is only when you actually sit down with a client and listen to what the issues and the problems are that you can start to apply intelligence and the skills of the designer to show how you can solve a problem.

SCHMIDLIN & PARTNER, REINACH, SWITZERLAND

Martin Amann, Stephan Nobs and Victor Mirabet

- In the beginning, we did no marketing at all, and we became very successful. Today, however, we find that we have to market ourselves in order to keep that success.

We are based in Reinach, near Basel, but our business in Switzerland only accounts for maybe 20 per cent of our turnover. We are pan-European, with our focus on Germany, Austria, Switzerland, Spain, Italy and Eastern Europe. We also cover France, but not as intensively as the other countries, and we are increasingly looking for business in the UK and Northern Europe, so we cover quite a wide area. We also take care of any international contacts which could provide business for GDN, Global Design Network, which has its headquarters in New York, but whose owners are from US, Canada, South America and Switzerland – that's us. We are responsible for the European part of the business. GDN also has companies in Taiwan, Japan, Denmark and London as cooperation partners, and we are currently thinking about contacts in the rest of the world.

In Switzerland, Schmidlin & Partner has created two new departments for the marketing task. The first is called marketing services, and they think about how to market Schmidlin and then go and do it. They create marketing brochures, case studies and slide presentations, and they manage the PR programme and our customer care programme. This contains all of the different planned activities to keep our current customers satisfied. The other department is called the new business department, and this prepares contacts with new client companies, basically by direct mail and on the telephone. They set up the meetings, and the rest is then up to us – mainly Stephan – to do the presentations and try to get new clients for Schmidlin. The most important thing about new business work is to do it as directly as possible, despite everything you see or read. We might prepare an approach with an opening letter, and then call afterwards, but we are just as likely to have seen something in a magazine, and just phone to try to make a presentation.

We shouldn't forget about PR, which is also a form of new business activity. It is not intended to be a direct form of marketing, but it can sometimes turn out to be that way. We give speeches at pan-European conferences, and we teach at different schools for young, professional marketing people, for example at the University of Basel and St Gallen. Sooner or later those people will come into the business, so we make presentations they won't forget. In five years, they might be at a point where they decide to remember us. We invest in long-term awareness of Schmidlin. With these activities, we also want to increase the general awareness of professional brand management and design solutions, and to show the importance of packaging in today's marketing mix.

We spend a lot of time on press relations, which we manage in-house. We make a short description of all of our projects as soon as they are on the market, and mail the details with photographs to between 30 and 50 publications. This is a regular publication which we send out every month, and we include whatever is ready. We have a design newsletter which we send out two or three times a year, which contains information about larger-scale projects we have done. We send this to about 4 000 clients and potential clients by using our own database which we have built up over the years. We also have a design journal which deals with branding issues and discusses one or two topics from the design world. Every action we do is automatically for both Schmidlin and GDN; we do not separate the two.

In Spain, Victor does his own marketing activities, based on general guidelines from the headquarters. Schmidlin & Partner Spain does more or less the same things, but PR is really very basic there. We do a lot of mailings, four times a year, of 3 000 newsletters containing case studies. In Southern European countries we are not so formal, we are more open and communication is better. We also look for new names through magazines, for example, and we constantly monitor new people and introduce them on to our databank. We analyse the market: for example we target potential clients with a minimum turnover and a minimum-sized marketing department and as soon as they reach a certain level, they will be on our list. Sometimes a client will ask an advertising agency to recommend a design company, so we also target advertising agencies by contacting them once a year, so they can see what we have done. Altogether, it's a combination of mailings, press releases and personal contact. In order to build up Spain, Victor did something like 150 presentations right at the beginning. To set up the dates, to do the presentations, it's a lot of work and a big investment, but if you want to start you've got to do it right, otherwise it won't work.

Throughout the company, we aim to achieve between 10 per cent to 15 per cent of our turnover from new clients each year as well as the current clientele which, of course, we try to keep. As a part of our customer care programme, we send out an evaluation sheet at the end of every project. You can usually tell if the client was genuinely happy and if they were sincere in their comments. If there are any doubts, we always call one or two months later and ask 'How was the opinion of sales?' or 'What was the impact of the new design?' or 'Do you have any Nielsen data yet?' It's very important to keep in contact even if you have a bad experience with clients. They have to feel that you are constantly in touch. Years ago, you could say: 'OK that project has finished, which is the next project?' Now, we have had to change. We have to say: 'This project has finished, but this is our customer,' so we have to take care of him, to always keep in contact.

We try to have annual meetings with our big clients to talk about past projects, future work and any improvements we can make. We can also offer different training seminars and workshops to companies, beginning with product innovation for new concepts to specific design training for product and brand managers, covering issues like 'non-verbal communication', 'how to judge design', 'how to brief your agency' etc. We have about seven different seminars and that gives us a regular platform for communicating with our clients, and for strengthening and improving in general our position as holistic brand and design consultants.

Of course, we have things like the presents we give to clients, like a bottle of champagne with a personal label, and our Christmas greetings card and so on. But the most important things when it comes to customer care are the evaluation sheets and taking personal care of clients.

SEYMOUR POWELL, LONDON, UK
Dick Powell

- In many ways, Seymour Powell is still a passion more than a business; the company is a life support system for the two partners.

It is much, much easier to see how you did it looking back than it was at the time. My partner Richard Seymour says that we are 'masters of the indirect sell'. In other words, we do not set off the equivalent of a block of dynamite in their faces. In my view, direct mail doesn't work. That is a blunderbuss approach when you really need a rifle, and preferably one with a telescopic sight.

We have no marketing people, no structure, although we do talk about changing that every two to three years. In 1984 we asked ourselves how to position ourselves against Ken Grange, AID and Conran – the big names at the time. Style was a filthy word then among industrial designers – so we sold style plus uncompromising quality. Our ten-year plan in 1984 was: 'If the Chairman of Sony was looking for a designer, ours would be one of the three names to come into his head.'

We set out to raise a profile for both ourselves and for the company. We had no track record, so we created in-house projects ourselves. We majored on PR and talked to everyone. We entered all of the competitions. Our objective was to get our foot in the door – potential clients would know who we were before we got in. What about abroad? The world was our market. Two years ago we had 100 per cent foreign clients, and no work from British companies at all. When we decided to start working in Japan, the first hurdle we had to overcome was cost; the flight alone was £1 500. We told clients that we would see other clients when there on a visit, so that in practice one financed the next. Our message had never been heard before, so we were battling on a fresh wicket; they bought it because they were curious. Generally, we limit both the amount of work we do and the size of the company to what we can design and manage in the time available, and we are quite relaxed about it.

What would I suggest to others? Develop an expertise over your competitors. Don't sell what clients can already do themselves; you will condemn yourselves for ever to working as an overload resource. Think about whom you would like to talk to, and research them so that you understand their products and their business. When you try to sell, the most critical thing is confidence in yourself, in your business and in what your business can do – but don't say you can do things which you can't. Lastly, never disappoint your clients, because you will lose them.

TAYBURN McILROY COATES, EDINBURGH, UK

Erick Davidson

• We have a little motto in Tayburn: treat our clients as we would close friends.

The best thing that anyone can do in marketing terms is to produce excellent creative work. People see what we have done for other organizations – other clients – and they are encouraged to believe that our company must be good, that we can do a good job for them. Hopefully they will then get on the phone to us! We try very hard in all cases to do really good creative work and, as far as we possibly can, link ourselves with that work. With printed literature, we put an imprint on it, although obviously you can't do that in many other respects, like on packaging. We then try to get good PR coverage, and we try to win awards. We also send actual products to clients who we think might be interested in something we've done, and point out why we have done it in a certain way and why it is unique or creative or different. Inevitably a lot of the marketing work we do is about name-dropping, and if you can say you've done things for BP and Shell and other major international companies – and for smaller ones which are relevant to that particular person – then people are reassured. They think 'Yes, if they have done such a good job for them, perhaps they can do a good job for us.'

We have three people who are specifically responsible for business development: one internationally, one on packaging and one on corporate. They cover all aspects of marketing – it's not just about ringing people up. It's much more about identifying opportunities through reading newspapers, having your ear to the grapevine, talking at conferences, being involved in PR, but most importantly being out there, networking in the wide world. In Scotland, that's a fairly easy thing to do: there are lots of organizations and you can get to know the bigger companies, and the individuals in them. I suppose that we are quite fortunate in that we are operating in a big way in a relatively small community. Our business is approximately 75 per cent Scottish, 10 per cent English, 15 per cent outside Britain, so Scotland continues to be a very important market for us.

We encourage everyone in the company to be a sales person and, to achieve that, you have to make sure that all your people are motivated. As well as looking after all our clients, we try to make sure that all our people are happy, because they are the best sales people we can have. This applies right from our switchboard and receptionist, who welcomes people with a smile and gets to know them; it all starts at the front door.

When we are out talking to potential clients, the way we present ourselves is more important than a good brochure. A lot of our business is about chemistry, and we always try to present ourselves as people who are energetic, enthusiastic, and who listen very carefully. We try to demonstrate that we care passionately about what we do – and we do care passionately. We are working in a very subjective area, and many clients find it hard to make calculated, logical assessments of why a piece of design is good or not good. They will often respond to design – and also to you – subjectively.

We also try to market ourselves very creatively, and try to find lateral solutions to things, so that we really get to people. We have done some very creative things over the years, either in the form of mailshots, or by literally getting ourselves into a position where we can meet an individual. They can be all sorts of things – like barbecues, or getting on planes. I once managed to sit next to someone on a shuttle from Edinburgh to London, just in order to spend an hour with him. I'd phoned him and phoned him and just hadn't got anywhere, and I actually managed to get in the seat next to him – that's quite tricky, I can assure you. He thought it was immensely funny and by the time we got to Heathrow we'd got the business. He was flattered that I'd gone to the trouble of buying a ticket just to sit next to him.

Sometimes, it's important just to push it; it's very hard to resist if someone phones you up 27 times. It demonstrates that you care, that they are not just a number on your database, and that you do actually want their business. It all comes back to that passion and enthusiasm, both in the sales approach and when you actually get to talk to someone. Generally, you need to listen. I have sat in meetings where someone has mentioned hearing about another opportunity, and if I see that we could be involved in that, I ask about it or follow it up later. You need to listen, and also to spot trends, economic trends, social trends. You need to focus your strength and energies on things which are expanding, on industrial sectors or even specific companies that are doing well, and to identify people in those companies who might be going places, who might be promoted, and then find an interesting way to approach them.

We don't have offices in other countries; our international work is mainly through strategic alliances, with architects or other companies abroad, or working with a foreign country's agent in this country. For example, we are doing some work in Norway, through a Norwegian agent. We are members of the British Design Initiative (BDI) which markets British design companies abroad, and we have picked up opportunities that way. International marketing is hard work, and it takes time and a lot of investment. We spent a lot of money three or four years ago setting up an office in Dubai, and we found it extremely difficult; nothing came out of it and we had spent a fortune. As I see it you have to spend years in the Middle East to try and create a position for yourself and become known.

We recently launched our interiors division as a separate company, Skakel and Skakel, in which we have a minority shareholding. We have divided the company into niche specialisms, so that we have a packaging company called The Branding Iron, a marketing and planning consultancy called Prism, and a tactical design company in Glasgow called Pointsize. We believe in specializing in a saturated marketplace. Our whole sector suffers from breakaways, and we try to recreate that energy and sense of purpose in a relatively small team – six or eight people working hard for each other has proved to be immensely successful for us. The person in charge of the operation has a sense of ownership and pride and feels great satisfaction when they win a piece of work. They can use the Tayburn Group name if they need to, they have our financial support and help, and can benefit from our technology services.

We are proud of our history of client retention. We average between 82 and 84 per cent a year in terms of number of retained clients, which I would like to think is pretty high. Our first four clients that we won when we started the business in 1979 are still with us. They have changed hugely as we have, but it's lovely to think that so many years later those organizations are still clients of ours. That's the best way to do business. Keeping the clients we have means really caring about them, treating them with trust and humour, not being officious or dogmatic, and treating them as individuals. We listen very carefully, and we look beyond the brief. It's easy to get a written brief and respond to it, but more difficult to think about it. As the old saying goes, thinking is very hard work, which is why so few people do it. You have to ask yourself what the real agenda is, what are people really trying to achieve – and that can spark creative, pro-active thinking.

In the future, I think that we are going to see more strategic alliances and more consortiums, and design companies are going to have to offer wider services than just pure design. These days, clients are looking for people who think creatively about communication. We are also seeing a much wider application of pro-active communication through technology such as the Internet, CDs etc – and that's going to be quite a challenge for most design companies. Any new companies starting up are going to have to find an innovative way of doing it. When we started, there were six design companies in Scotland. Currently there are 367. There's simply no point in launching another 'me-too'. You have to have an immense talent or an approach to your product and business that no one else has thought of – and, believe me, that is difficult.